THE *Private Life* OF
ELVIS

pil

Publications International, Ltd.

Richard Buskin is *The New York Times* best-selling author of more than a dozen books on subjects ranging from Marilyn Monroe and Princess Diana to The Beatles and Sheryl Crow—in 2005, he coauthored the autobiography of comic Phyllis Diller. His articles have appeared in newspapers such as the *New York Post,* the *Sydney Morning Herald,* the *Observer,* and the *Independent,* and he also writes features and reviews for film and music magazines around the world. A native of London, England, he now lives in Chicago.

Consultant: Susan Doll, Ph.D.

Special thanks to Bill Burk, *Elvis World Magazine;* Lea Frydman, www.elvispresleynews.com; and Joseph Krein, www.elvis2001.net.

Quotation from *TV GUIDE®* magazine courtesy of TV Guide Magazine Group, Inc. "©1956 TV Guide Magazine Group, Inc."

Photo credits:

Front cover:
AP Wide World Photos (bottom left center); **Sharon Fox/Sam Griffith** (bottom left); **Heavenlea Productions** (top left, top center & top right); **Joseph A. Krein** (bottom right center); **PIL Collection** (bottom center & bottom right).

Back cover:
Sharon Fox/Sam Griffith (top); **Heavenlea Productions** (bottom).

AP Wide World Photos: 7 (left), 9, 11 (bottom), 12, 34, 35, 36 (top), 37, 40 (top), 41, 51, 58 (bottom), 59, 61, 75 (top), 87; Getty Images, 11 (top), 16, 28; National Archives, 93; **Bill Burk:** 15, 17, 18, 19, 53, 58 (top), 66 (bottom), 67 (bottom), 69, 73, 75 (bottom), 92 (bottom), 94; June Juanico, 55; Bob Klein, 92 (top); **Sharon Fox:** Dave Szarzak/White Eagle, 83; **Getty Images:** 38, 40 (bottom), 42, 56 (top), 57, 76, 78; AFP, 44, 84; Time Life Pictures, 23, 39 (bottom), 43, 45, 48, 49, 50; **Heavenlea Productions:** 6, 7 (right), 10, 13, 21, 22, 24, 25, 26, 33, 39 (top), 46, 56 (bottom), 62, 64, 66 (top), 67 (top), 77, 79, 81 (top), 85, 89, 90; **Joseph A. Krein:** 30, 31, 81 (bottom), 82, 86; **Roger Marshutz/Motion Picture & TV Archive:** 14; **PIL Collection:** 20, 32, 36 (bottom), 60, 71; **SuperStock:** 47; Steve Vidler, 29.

Louis Weber, CEO
Publications International, Ltd.
7373 North Cicero Avenue
Lincolnwood, Illinois 60712

Permission is never granted for commercial purposes.

ISBN-13: 978-1-4127-2192-9
ISBN-10: 1-4127-2192-X

Manufactured in China.

8 7 6 5 4 3 2 1

Contents

The Man Behind the Image

"An image is one thing, a human being is another. It's very hard to live up to an image."
Elvis Presley, 1972

It's hardly surprising that so much has been written about Elvis Aaron Presley. One of the 20th century's most phenomenal singers, he was blessed with a rare combination of talent, killer

Elvis had a close relationship with his parents, Vernon and Gladys Presley.

looks, and magnetic charm. His legendary career, with its attendant controversies and widespread acclaim,

afforded him extraordinary fame and unprecedented success. His rags-to-riches life story featured all the classic elements: a meteoric rise to fame, an opulent lifestyle, excessive habits, and a tragic, overtly public demise.

Many of the words committed to print have pertained to Elvis's music, and since his death even more have focused on the more salacious and tawdry aspects of his action-packed existence. This book, however, takes another direction. Neither a straightforward biography nor a scandal-filled exposé, it largely circumvents Elvis's music and film careers in order to provide an insightful and respectful behind-the-scenes glimpse into the private life of the King of Rock 'n' Roll.

The chapters adhere to specific themes rather than to a strict chronology, and they cover a variety of different topics. You will see how Elvis's poverty-stricken childhood helped him to form a remarkably strong relationship with his parents; how the pressures of fame led him to seek out the serenity of Graceland; and how he indulged his own needs and desires while satisfying those of others. You'll get an intimate look at several facets of Elvis's life, including his relationships with friends and girlfriends, his time in the Army, life with Priscilla, and even his quest for a satisfying spiritual life.

Elvis was a man of wild contradictions: a reclusive thinker who could rarely be alone; a loving friend whose constant

Elvis shares a loving moment with his daughter, Lisa Marie.

Anita Wood was Elvis's girlfriend in the late 1950s.

need for female company undid any serious relationships that he pursued with the opposite sex; and a religious, spiritual

being who succumbed to the excesses of the material world. Nevertheless, Elvis Presley's legacy lies not only in his great recordings and the pleasure that he brought—and still brings—to millions of people, but also in the way that he changed the lives of all who knew him.

No one looked like Elvis, walked like Elvis, talked like Elvis, smiled like Elvis, dressed like Elvis, moved like Elvis, or, indeed, sang like Elvis—the man was unforgettable, irreplaceable, unique. As Bruce Springsteen said in 1977, "There have been a lotta tough guys. There have been pretenders. There have been contenders. But there is only one King."

Young Dreams

As a child, Elvis knew all about poverty and struggle, yet his parents' love and his passion for music would see him through.

One hundred miles southeast of his future mansion in Memphis, Tennessee, Elvis Aaron Presley entered the world in East Tupelo, Mississippi, in the early morning hours of January 8, 1935. The two-room shotgun shack where Elvis was born was light-years away from Graceland in all respects. The term "shotgun shack" describes a house so tiny, a bullet fired through its front entrance can fly straight through the house without hitting anything. The Presley home was, in a word, basic, and so were its immediate surroundings.

Located above a highway that transported locals between Tupelo and Birmingham, Alabama, and nestled among a group of small, rough-hewn homes along Old Saltillo Road, Elvis's birthplace was built by his father, Vernon, with help from Vernon's brother Vester and father, Jessie, whose relatively "spacious" four-room house sat next door. These were the humblest of beginnings. In the mid–1930s, in the middle of

the Great Depression, East Tupelo was a haven for poor sharecroppers and factory workers—as well as assorted bootleggers and prostitutes—whose meager resources still largely outstripped those of Elvis's parents. Not only did Vernon and his wife, Gladys, rely on welfare to pay the $15 that Dr. William Robert Hunt charged for delivering Elvis and his stillborn twin brother, Jesse Garon, but neighbors and friends also had to provide them with diapers.

Confusion over the correct spelling of Elvis's middle name has existed since Dr. Hunt logged the name "Evis Aaron Presley" in his ledger after the birth. The birth certificate issued by the state of Mississippi shows the spelling "Aron," which is also found on his draft notice. Elvis's gravestone in the Meditation Gardens at Graceland, however, is engraved with the more common spelling "Aaron." Alternate spellings of names were typical in the era of the Depression, particularly in rural communities where educational opportunities were limited and the writ-

The two-room shotgun shack where Elvis was born has evolved from a modest dwelling to a major tourist attraction, complete with a museum, memorial chapel, and gift shop.

ten word was less significant than it is now. Since the Presleys chose Elvis's middle name to honor their friend and church songleader Aaron Kennedy, who was himself a twin, it is likely that "Aaron" was the intended spelling.

Before Elvis was born, Gladys earned $2 a day at the Tupelo Garment Company, while Vernon worked at various odd jobs, including one on the dairy farm of Orville S. Bean. With $180 that he borrowed from Bean after Gladys became pregnant in the spring of 1934, Vernon set about constructing a family home,

and he and Gladys moved in that December. Today, as part of a tourist attraction that includes a small museum, memorial chapel, gift shop, and wooded park on the renamed Elvis Presley Drive, the house that Vernon Presley built looks markedly different than when the future King of Rock 'n' Roll first tested his vocal cords there.

While the ceiling and roof of this Mississippi landmark have been replaced, the basic structure still stands, yet the wood exterior is now painted, the front porch has a swing, and the interior has been

The bond between Elvis and his mother, shown here circa 1946, was extraordinarily strong. Around this time, Gladys bought Elvis his first guitar.

where Gladys kept a flock of chickens and a cow.

Although material goods weren't readily available during his early years, Elvis never lacked the one thing that is most important to any child: the love of his parents. Vernon was a dedicated father and Gladys adored her only child, forming a bond that was so close, it extended to lifelong baby talk between the two, such as Elvis calling her by the pet name of Satnin'. Scared to let him out of her sight, Gladys accompanied Elvis everywhere, including the tiny First Assembly of God Church, where her uncle Gains Mansell was the preacher and where Elvis got his first real taste of music. At age two, he would slide off his mother's lap, climb onto the platform in front of the 25-strong congregation, and stand before the choir, trying to sing along even though he was too young to know the words to the hymns.

Another place that mother and son regularly visited was the Priceville Cemetery, where Jesse Garon was buried in an unmarked grave. Although bolstered by Gladys's belief that, as reported in a September 1956 issue of *TV Guide,* "when one twin died, the one that lived got all the strength of both," Elvis grew up in his brother's shadow. Nevertheless, he was always mindful of Jessie's ghostly presence watching over him, ensuring

embellished with period furniture, wallpaper, curtains, and electrical appliances such as a sewing machine that the Presley family could never have afforded when they lived there. Forget the radio that now sits in the living room; the home was originally lit with oil lamps because it wasn't hooked up to the town's electric system. The nicely landscaped front yard is a far cry from the dirt patch

This Presley family tombstone is located in Tupelo's Priceville Cemetery, where Elvis and his mother paid regular visits to the unmarked grave of his stillborn twin brother, Jesse Garon.

that he tried to do the right thing. This, together with the special confidence he shared with his mother, encouraged an insular quality that Elvis would retain to the end of his days. Many who knew him, including his wife, Priscilla, have attested to a loneliness that no one could resolve, and while this side of Elvis was greatly exacerbated following Gladys's death during his early twenties, it stemmed from a childhood in which he often retreated into his own little world—a world defined by a strong attachment to his mother and the florid thoughts of his fertile imagination.

A Hometown Boy Makes Good

In January 1971, the United States Junior Chamber of Commerce (the Jaycees) named Elvis Presley one of the Ten Outstanding Young Men of the Nation for 1970. During a prayer breakfast, Elvis (with wife Priscilla by his side) received a round of applause from the assembled crowd. At the awards ceremony, which was held in Memphis, Elvis made a speech that touched on his early aspirations: "When I was a child, ladies and gentlemen, I was a dreamer. I read comic books, and I was the hero of the comic book. I saw movies, and I was the hero in the movie. So every dream that I ever dreamed has come true a hundred times."

Vernon Presley was incarcerated in the Mississippi State Penitentiary at Parchman for his involvement in altering and cashing a check. Elvis and Gladys often made the ten-hour round-trip by bus to visit him on weekends.

Life was fairly settled during Elvis's first three years. He and his parents formed a tight-knit trio, rarely socializing or venturing far from the family home—but everything changed in May 1938 after Vernon went to prison for his part in altering and cashing a check he received from Orville Bean.

Vernon was indicted for forgery, along with Travis Smith and Luther Gable, and sentenced to three years at the Mississippi State Penitentiary. He served only eight months of his sentence, but during that time Bean repossessed the Presley home, forcing Gladys and Elvis to move into a couple of temporary homes: next door with Vernon's parents, and then on

Maple Street in Tupelo, where they lived with Gladys's cousins Frank and Leona Richards.

If this was a difficult period for Vernon, it wasn't much easier for his wife and son. Gladys struggled—and sometimes failed—to make ends meet taking in laundry and working as a seamstress, while Elvis suffered through the realization of the separation anxiety that he felt with regard to his father.

Elvis was extremely afraid of losing his father. When the family went swimming, Elvis didn't want Vernon to dive for fear that something bad would happen to him. In another instance, a neighbor's house caught fire, and Vernon rushed inside to help save their belongings. Gladys reportedly had to hold her distraught son back from going in after his father. Elvis cried and screamed at the possibility that Vernon could get hurt, and Gladys had to reassure him by telling him sharply to trust that Vernon knew what he was doing.

That last comment wouldn't have reassured the child in 1938, when many of his worst fears came true. His only respite came in the form of those weekends when Gladys and Elvis made the five-hour bus journey to visit Vernon in the Mississippi State Penitentiary at Parchman. The ten-hour round-trip—which they made all in one day—presumably solidified the mother-son union more than ever.

When Vernon was released in February 1939, a month after Elvis's fourth birthday, Gladys and Elvis were still living with Frank and Leona Richards on Maple Street. Before long, however, they were back in East Tupelo and, following a brief stay with Vernon's older brother Vester (who was married to Gladys's sister Clettes), living in a succession of low-rent homes.

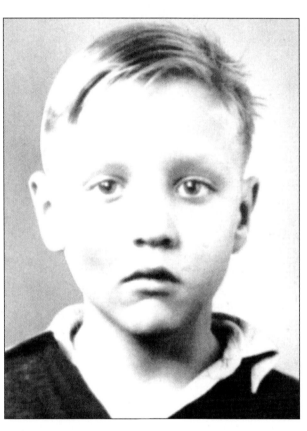

As a small child, Elvis displayed the beginnings of his famous curled upper lip.

One of the few constants in Elvis's life around this time was the First Assembly of God Church, where he and his parents sang in the choir, as well as Lawhon Elementary School on Lake Street, which he began attending in the fall of 1941. Already a loner, used to playing on his own more than with his few friends, Elvis soon learned to read, and he would while away hours on end with his small collection of comic books. He also became reacquainted with his father's absence. Benefiting from increased work opportunities created by America's entry into World War II, the Presleys relocated to the Mississippi Gulf Coast where Vernon and his cousin Sales found employment in the Moss Point Shipyard near Pascagoula in

September 26, 1956, was proclaimed "Elvis Presley Day" in Tupelo, and the hometown hero performed two concerts there at the Mississippi–Alabama Fair and Dairy Show, where he'd made his first public appearance just over a decade earlier. This time, a hundred National Guard troops were called in to control the crowd.

1940. The relocation was short-lived. Missing their family and friends, Vernon and Gladys returned to East Tupelo about a month later. Vernon spent most of 1942 living apart from his family in Mississippi, Alabama, and finally in Memphis, Tennessee, where he worked in a munitions plant while returning to East Tupelo to be with Elvis and Gladys on weekends.

Vernon saved enough money by the war's end to make a $200 down payment on a four-room, $2,000 house on Berry Street. Amazingly, the person selling him the property was none other than Orville Bean, whose altered check

had previously landed Vernon in jail. And shortly afterward it was Bean's daughter, Oleta Grimes, who encouraged Elvis to make his very first public performance, competing in a radio talent contest on Children's Day at the annual Mississippi–Alabama Fair and Dairy Show in downtown Tupelo. Grimes, who also happened to be Elvis's fifth-grade teacher, was impressed by his singing during morning prayers. Legend has it that, wearing glasses and standing on a chair to reach the microphone in front of several hundred people, Elvis won second place by crooning, without accompaniment, "Old Shep," the Red Foley tearjerker about a boy's dear, departed dog. Elvis's prize supposedly consisted of free passes for all of the rides at the fair plus five dollars.

Research done by Bill Burk for his book *Early Elvis: The Tupelo Years* has dispelled this myth. Interviews with Elvis's family and friends, as well as comments made by Elvis himself, confirm that he did sing "Old Shep" without accompaniment, and that he did wear glasses for a short time in the fifth grade. However, he did not place second at the fair. He may have placed fifth, but probably did not win a prize.

Elvis's lack of musical accompaniment was soon resolved when his mother bought him a guitar from the Tupelo Hardware Company for his eleventh (or possibly tenth, according to some versions of the story) birthday. Gladys saw it as a cheap and safe alternative to the bicycle that Elvis originally requested. Taught different chords by his Uncle Vester, Elvis began singing and playing in church and on the WELO *Saturday Jamboree,* a popular radio talent show broadcast from the local courthouse.

The WELO *Jamboree* brought Elvis his first direct contact with show business. Mississippi Slim, whose real name was Carvel Lee Ausborn, was the star of the show, combining country music with comedy, and he not only backed Elvis on guitar but also taught him new chords and songs. Slim's younger brother, James Ausborn, was in Elvis's class at East Tupelo Consolidated, and sometimes, the boys would visit Slim at the studio of radio station WELO, where he had his own midday show. That way, Elvis would get a further opportunity to gain instruction on what to sing and how to play.

Inspired by the country music he heard on the radio from the Grand Ole Opry every Saturday night, as well as the gospel-flavored sounds ringing around church each Sunday morning, Elvis was filled with a hunger to learn and a yen for hanging around musicians such as Slim, who apparently knew some of the *big* stars, such as singing cowboy Tex Ritter. Yet no one, including Elvis, could

Elvis attended Milam Junior High School in Tupelo until his family moved to Memphis just after he started eighth grade. He often brought his guitar to school and played for his classmates.

Vernon, Gladys, and Elvis stand in front of their East Tupelo home, circa 1941. Already a loner, Elvis would while away hours reading comic books.

have guessed that he'd already embarked on the path that would lead him to fame and fortune.

In the summer of 1946, unable to afford the payments on their Berry Street house, Elvis and his parents moved out of East Tupelo into the neighboring city of Tupelo, and soon found themselves living on its version of Poverty Row. Mulberry Alley was located opposite Shake Rag,

Tupelo's black quarter, and the Presleys' home there was little more than a hovel. A half-mile away was Milam Junior High School, where Elvis entered sixth grade in the fall. An average student, he was far too withdrawn to make much of an impression on either his teachers or his classmates. Only when he began to bring his guitar to school in seventh grade to play during lunch would that situation change.

In the meantime, Elvis and his family changed addresses as frequently as Vernon changed jobs. Between Vernon's earnings—although unambitious, he was rarely unemployed—the pay that Gladys received for working at the Mid-South Laundry, and money from a series of loans, they were able to keep their heads above water, and by the second half of 1947 the Presleys were living on North Green Street, located in a "colored" neighborhood. Consequently looked down upon by several of his white class-mates, Elvis must have also been regarded as an intruder within the local black community, yet he was drawn like a magnet to the music that he heard on the streets, around the churches, and coming out of the clubs and bars. It was earthy, it was wild, and above all, it was exciting, reflecting the participants' col-orful clothes, manner of speech, and in certain cases, mode of behavior. For a poor boy with limited communication skills but expansive dreams and an open mind, it must have been an exhilarating experience.

Through seventh and eighth grades, Elvis showed up at Milam Junior High School every day with his guitar, playing it for anyone who cared to listen in the basement recess area during lunch, and he began embellishing his performances with strains of what was commonly known as "race music." For many of his schoolmates this was a turnoff—a few even made their point by cutting his guitar strings—yet others at least turned an ear toward his vocalizing of country standards. No one knew they were witnessing the birth of a legend. And no one really seemed upset when they learned that he was moving to Memphis.

Perpetually out of money and by now out of reasons to remain in Tupelo, Vernon and Gladys decided it was time to make a new start across the state line in Tennessee. So they sold their few bits of furniture, loaded up their Plymouth with clothes and other belongings, and never looked back. In Memphis, they initially lived in a rooming house on Washington Street and then another on Poplar Avenue, eating and sleeping in a single room while sharing a bathroom with three other families in a sixteen-unit house. Vernon, who worked at a series of factory jobs, applied for public housing

to improve their situation, and his request was answered in September 1949 when the Memphis Housing Authority moved the family into an apartment at nearby Lauderdale Courts, in the northern part of the city. The $35 monthly rent was a dollar more than it cost to live on Poplar Avenue, and the place itself was run-down and in need of repair, but at least the Presleys now had enough space to move, with a living room, kitchen, two bedrooms, and a private bathroom.

Lauderdale Courts, with its lively assortment of young families, was located close

Even as a teenager, Elvis had a well-defined personal style—here he strikes a nonchalant pose against a late-1940s model Lincoln.

Standing in front of the Presleys' Lauderdale Courts apartment wearing earmuffs, Elvis tries to show that he's quick on the draw.

to downtown attractions, such as the stores and movie theaters along Main Street, as well as the clubs and bars along Beale Street. By most standards, this was a bustling community; to a wide-eyed 14-year-old accustomed to the figuratively duller lights of Tupelo it was probably nothing short of awe inspiring.

Here were all the elements to fire a teenager's imagination, as well as the

means to help realize his ambitions, musical or otherwise. At this point, it's not clear quite what Elvis's ambitions were, except that he hoped to one day earn enough money to afford an easier life for himself and his family. Starting out in yet another school, he didn't share his musical hobby with his new classmates at L. C. Humes High School, where he majored in industrial arts/woodshop. But he did feel free enough to play the guitar and sing around a trio of boys with whom he became fast friends.

Farley Guy, Paul Dougher, and Buzzy Forbess all lived at Lauderdale Courts, and together they and Elvis went to the movies, swam, played football, wandered downtown, and even earned money mowing yards with a push mower purchased by Vernon. Farley, Paul, and Buzzy were aware of Elvis's interest in music, and so were his parents. Vernon, Gladys, and Elvis often spent time gathered around the radio together to hear country acts like Eddy Arnold, Sleepy Eyed John, and the Louvin Brothers; and gospel groups like the Blackwood Brothers and Elvis's personal favorites, the Statesmen. Led by the charismatic Jake Hess, this quartet's flamboyant clothes and highly stylized singing made a deep impression on the young Elvis. Musical and cultural influences were bombarding him from all directions, and he was soaking them up like a sponge.

Elvis formed a close friendship with a trio of boys who, like him, lived at Lauderdale Courts and attended L. C. Humes High School. From left: *Farley Guy, Elvis, Paul Dougher, and Buzzy Forbess.*

By the time Elvis was in tenth grade at Humes High, he had hooked up with another group of teenagers living in Lauderdale Courts: Lee Denson and Johnny Black, and brothers Dorsey and Johnny Burnette. The foursome had a loose-knit musical group that performed country standards outdoors for the residents on balmy summer evenings, and Elvis joined in to contribute background

The Memphis Music Scene

A wide variety of music was available in Memphis during the early 1950s via radio stations such as WMPS, WDIA, and WHBQ. WDIA was owned by a couple of white men, Bert Ferguson and John R. Pepper, who employed black disc jockeys to spin blues records, especially those by local artists. Another white station, WHBQ, also wasn't averse to broadcasting "race records," as evidenced on *Red Hot and Blue,* the show of disc jockey Dewey Phillips, who specialized in playing the rhythm-and-blues material of black artists. Dewey would soon play a vital role in the early success of Elvis Presley, introducing him to Southern audiences by playing his records in heavy rotation.

The Presleys relocated several times during Elvis's childhood. They lived in an apartment in Lauderdale Courts from 1949 until 1952.

vocals. His growing musical confidence also began to attract female attention, including that of early girlfriends such as Betty McMahan and Billie Wardlaw, both of whom lived in the Courts. Others at Humes High encountered an altogether different Elvis—both in terms of appearance and demeanor—during his junior year of high school, 1951.

At a time when certain rhythm-and-blues recordings—most notably, Jackie Brenston's "Rocket 88"—closely resembled what would soon be known as rock 'n' roll, Elvis began melding the music's sensuous, carefree attitude with the look of a roughneck truck driver: long, greased-down hair and sideburns that were at odds with his invariably polite manners. His appearance garnered much

attention, and some of the rougher boys at school responded by threatening to beat him up and cut his hair. One legend that has been passed around for many years is that Elvis was even kicked off the school football team for refusing to change his look by cutting his long hair. The truth of the matter was much less dramatic. Although Coach Rube Boyce did ask Elvis at one point to get a haircut, Elvis quit the football team of his own accord. In interviews with Bill Burk given for *Early Elvis: The Humes Years,* both Coach Boyce and Assistant Coach Malcolm Phillips recalled that Elvis quit the team because he got an after-school job. Shortly after he left the team, Elvis began to wear what would later become his trademark flashy clothes—usually an eye-catching combination of pink and black—that he bought with the earnings from his part-time job as an usher at Loew's State Theater on South Main Street.

As Elvis's passion for music became all-consuming, his schoolwork faltered. An assortment of A, B, and C grades during his freshman year at Humes had degenerated to the point where he was a straight-C student. He spent much of his free time going to the movies and hanging out in record stores. He also attended all-night gospel singing sessions with his parents at the Ellis Auditorium, where he would observe some of the more extroverted performers' animated stage movements. Gospel encapsulated the spirituality and physicality that was at the center of Elvis Presley's musical style, yet when he sang and played guitar at parties he was more likely to croon a pop number by Dean Martin, Bing Crosby, or Perry Como.

By the end of 1952, the Presleys' combined income exceeded the maximum allowed by the Memphis Housing Authority, so the family moved from Lauderdale Courts to a rooming house on nearby Saffarans Street, and then an apartment at 462 Alabama Street, opposite the Courts. Though the Presleys were forced to leave the housing project, they chose to remain in the same neighborhood. However, Elvis was about to move in a new direction.

This photo of Elvis was featured in the L. C. Humes High School yearbook, The Herald.

In April 1953, a couple of months before he graduated from high school, Elvis performed in Humes's annual Minstrel Show. Sixteenth on a 22-act bill, listed in the program as "Elvis Prestly," he shocked pupils, parents, and teachers alike with his performance of Teresa Brewer's "Till I Waltz Again with You." It was a seminal moment. Like a scene out of one of his future movies, Elvis set aside his own shy personality in favor of a popular and animated persona, and the peculiar-looking young man began to attract the attention of his peers like moths to a flame.

After graduating from L. C. Humes High School, Elvis went to work for M. B. Parker Machinists—hardly the stuff of legends. However, the fates were conspiring in his favor, the pieces were falling into place, and soon all of Elvis Presley's dreams would come true.

"Baby Let's Play House"

Once he achieved superstardom, the world that Elvis inhabited was the polar opposite to all he had known before. He indulged his every whim, yet he stayed close to his geographical roots.

Elvis was working for M. B. Parker Machinists Shop in the summer of 1953, when he spent $4 to record his first songs—he covered two songs by the Ink Spots, "My Happiness" and "That's When Your Heartaches Begin"—at Sam Phillips's Memphis Recording Service. It was money well spent, as Elvis's income skyrocketed dur-ing the first few months of 1956, when his life was a nonstop whirl of concert performances, recording sessions, and TV appearances. However, it wasn't until March of that year, when his debut single for RCA Records, "Heartbreak Hotel," was heading toward the top of the U.S. charts, that he and his parents moved from their apartment into a home befitting his status as music's hottest new artist.

Vernon and Gladys pose proudly alongside their son's growing fleet of cars (and Harley-Davidson) at their home on Audubon Drive.

The house at 1034 Audubon Drive, located in an upscale residential neighborhood east of downtown Memphis, afforded the Presleys their first real taste of the good life. Elvis paid $40,000—a sizable chunk of change in 1956—for the pastel-green, wood-frame, seven-room ranch house. He listed himself and his parents on the title as co-owners, and he quickly had a swimming pool and changing room installed in the backyard, next to the carport that accommodated his Harley-Davidson motorcycle and growing collection of automobiles. Typical of his lifestyle at this pivotal stage in his career, Elvis was touring when his parents moved into the house with Vernon's mother, Minnie Mae. Each time Elvis came home, he brought chairs, lamps, or other items that he'd purchased on the road, prompting an anxious Gladys, forever concerned about his safety, to suggest that her son should settle down with a wife and kids and open his own furniture store.

For his part, Elvis presented his mother with two electric mixers, one for each end of the kitchen. Gladys still prepared his favorite foods when he was home. He also hired a maid to help with the household chores. In all other respects, this was a typical Eisenhower-era American home—except, perhaps, for the many music awards hanging on the living

Elvis bought a pair of electric mixers, one for each end of the kitchen at Audubon Drive, so that his mother would never have to walk too far to reach one.

room wall and the fans who came to visit at all hours.

While Audubon Drive's teens were thrilled to be living next to a national star, many neighbors were less than enamored with the fan mania surrounding the Presley home. The home was soon transformed into one of Memphis's chief tourist attractions when Elvis was home. Kids would line up from dawn until dusk for autographs, a chat, a glimpse of Elvis, or mementos such as grass or pool water. There were even street vendors selling popcorn. This, added to the sight of Gladys hanging her washing on the line and a steady stream of relatives popping in for a visit, was too much for several of the residents. The Presley family often went out of their way to be nice to neighbors and fans alike, but some neighbors made their feelings clear by bringing a lawsuit against them for creating a public nuisance. The magistrate ruled that the fans' behavior was neither Elvis's fault nor his responsibility. Several of the neighbors tried to purchase Elvis's new house, and he responded by offering to buy *all* of their homes. It soon became obvious that the house on Audubon Drive was ill-equipped to handle the hoopla that constantly surrounded Elvis.

Elvis was very gracious toward his fans, and sometimes spent hours in front of the house signing autographs and chatting with them. They were, after all, the reason for his success, and throughout the rest of his life he never failed to appreciate this. Concerned, as ever, for her son's well-being, Gladys would call his name repeatedly until he went inside for his supper, and she'd also chase away early-morning visitors who might disrupt his much-needed rest. Eventually, even Elvis grew tired of the constant invasion of privacy at the family's home on Audubon Drive. So, in March 1957, while he was in Hollywood filming his second movie, *Loving You,*

The "Memphis Kid" takes a break during filming of his second movie, Loving You. *Elvis's character, Deke—a truck driver with a natural talent for singing—was based on his real-life experiences.*

The Yuletide season was always special for Elvis, who ensured that elaborate decorations turned Graceland into a winter wonderland.

Gladys and Vernon began searching for a larger, more secluded home, and they quickly found the property with which their son would be forever associated.

Situated on 13.8 lush, wooded acres in Whitehaven, close to the two-lane Highway 51 that connected Memphis with Jackson, Mississippi, Graceland was an 18-room colonial estate set on a hilltop and surrounded by sycamores, weeping willows, magnolias, and sweet gums, with a row of pin oaks leading up to the house. Boasting a neoclassical facade, its front door framed by four columns, this modest mansion appealed to Elvis at first sight: It was a place that would symbolize his success yet still offer the warmth and intimacy of a real home, in a location that provided seclusion yet was only a few miles south of downtown Memphis. Without hesitation he agreed to pay the seller, Mrs. Ruth Moore, about $100,000 for the house and grounds.

No sooner had Elvis and his family moved into Graceland in April 1957 than the renovations began. First he had the

Songs for Gladys?

Rock 'n' roll legend has it that Elvis was a talented but inexperienced singer when he made his first trip into the recording studio to make a record for his mother's birthday in 1953. Given Elvis's strong attachment to Gladys, and her unwavering belief in her son, this version of the story would be easy to accept....except that Gladys Presley's birthday is in April, and Elvis didn't make his recordings until late summer. The more likely explanation is that Elvis came to the Memphis Recording Service to catch the attention of Sam Phillips, an independent producer who was rumored to be looking for a talented artist who could adapt rhythm-and-blues music for a more mainstream audience.

entire property surrounded by an eight-foot-high pink Alabama fieldstone wall at a cost of $65,000, while iron gates at the entrance to the driveway, embellished with music notes and a hip-swiveling guitarist designed by Abe Saucer, were custom-built and installed by John Dillars, Sr., for a mere $2,400. The music notes on the gates are said to represent the opening bars of "Love Me Tender."

Next up was a chicken coop for Gladys, a bean-shaped swimming pool, and an extended patio to accommodate visits from family and friends. Aided by interior decorator George Golden, Elvis reportedly spent upward of $500,000 on Graceland during his first year there, creating a beautiful bedroom for his mother, an eight-foot-square bed for himself, a fifteen-foot sofa for the living room, and a soda fountain for his friends. And that was only the beginning.

Thanks to all the additions made over the years, the house was expanded from 10,266 square feet to 17,552 square feet (excluding the 2,240-square-foot racquetball court that Elvis commissioned to indulge his latest hobby in 1975). It contained 23 rooms, including eight bathrooms. Today, a

tour of America's second most visited home (after the White House) provides the public with a glimpse of much, but not all, of the property, while approximating its appearance not at the time of Elvis's death—when several rooms were decked out in bright red carpet, curtains, and walls—but at various periods of the 1960s and the early '70s.

A tour of Graceland offers insight into Elvis's private life. Inside Graceland's front door is the foyer where Elvis's casket lay in state after his passing in August 1977, and directly above is the bathroom where he died. While the dining room, living room, music room, and kitchen are all interesting first-floor attractions, the true stunner, revealing the King's excesses, is the den.

Gladys Presley's health was fading, but her devotion to her son (and his for his mother) never wavered.

Nicknamed the "jungle room" by tour guides, this room started life as a screened-in porch before being enclosed during the early '60s. An indoor waterfall was added in 1965. However, things really took off in 1974 when, during a 30-minute shopping spree at Donald's Furniture store in Memphis, Elvis kitted out the room with some of the gaudiest furniture ever seen. The room features Polynesian-style chairs upholstered with fake fur, as well as matching bar, stools, tables, and cabinet, all boasting elaborate animal-head features and totem-style engravings carved out of wood. A huge "monkey chair" actually necessitated the removal of a window in order to get it into the room.

Wood paneling, together with green shag carpeting on the floor and ceiling, and a mirror framed with pheasant and peacock feathers, complete the jungle room's fun—if somewhat tacky—effect. While all this serves to reinforce Elvis's strong affinity for Hawaii, there is some debate as to what actually motivated his choice of decor. One version of events has Vernon commenting on the repulsive furniture that he'd seen in a store named Donald's, and Elvis deciding to poke fun at his money-conscious father by spending a small fortune in that particular establishment. A more straightforward explanation is that, impressed by what he'd seen when visiting Hawaii's Polyne-

sian Cultural Center, the King simply wanted to remind himself of his favorite vacation destination, which he'd popularized with two movies, a concert broadcast live via satellite, and numerous songs. The truth may lie somewhere in between. What is known is that all of the carpeting and wood paneling gave the jungle room such favorable acoustics that Elvis recorded the better part of two albums there: *From Elvis Presley Boulevard, Memphis Tennessee*—which referred to the renamed Highway 51—and more than half of *Moody Blue*. (The furniture was removed for these recording sessions.)

While many of the personal spaces at Graceland—including Elvis's bedroom, bathroom, wardrobe room, and office; a guest bath and dressing area; and daughter Lisa Marie's bedroom and bathroom—are off-limits to the public, Gladys Presley's bedroom was opened to the public on Mother's Day, 1998. The room was restored to its appearance at the time of her death 40 years earlier, when the white walls, carpet, and furniture served as an elegant backdrop for the deep purple of the bedding and drapes.

There is plenty more pizzazz following a walk down a mirrored staircase into the basement area. The TV room features a bank of three televisions set in a wall unit, as well as a 1950s jukebox filled with Elvis's personal record collection.

The walls, ceiling, fireplace, and bar are covered in mirrors. The pool room, a dazzling mix of styles, including a large lamp by Laukhuff Stained Glass, is dominated by a huge pool table and draped in nearly 400 yards of patchwork-print fabric that covers the ceiling and walls in spectacular fashion. Since the jungle room, TV room, and pool room makeovers all took place in 1974, along with the carpeting and drapery that heralded his "red period," it's clear that this was a particularly busy year for Elvis the decorator.

Just south of the main house at Graceland is the building that houses the trophy room, a collection of memorabilia and awards that run the gamut from priceless to eccentric. Elvis's many gold and platinum records and countless other musical awards are displayed in the 80-foot-long "Hall of Gold," while other treasures in the trophy room include Elvis's grade school achievement tests, the wedding outfits worn by Elvis and Priscilla, various gifts sent by fans, and, of course, a collection of jeweled jumpsuits from the 1970s.

Graceland is second only to the White House as America's most visited home. One of the first sights to greet guests when they enter Elvis's home is the plush white living room to the right of the main entrance.

Plenty of Elvis memorabilia is on display at Graceland, from gold records and show costumes to his gun collection and Army uniform.

Among the most visited sites at Graceland is the Meditation Garden. Constructed in 1966, the Meditation Garden was inspired by the Self-Realization Fellowship Center's Lake Shrine in Pacific Palisades, California, which Elvis visited as part of his ongoing spiritual quest. It was intended as a place within the grounds of his home where he could think alone and find some measure of peace. The garden features a 12-foot circular pool with 14 different sprays and colored underwater lighting, backed by a curved brick wall with four stained glass windows imported from Spain. Eight columns set in a semicircle in front of the wall support a wooden trellis, and at their center stands a statue of Jesus presented to Elvis by his close friends.

Although it was never intended as a burial site, the Meditation Garden is the final resting place of Elvis and Gladys. Their bodies were moved from Forest Hills Cemetery and reinterred here in October 1977 at the request of Vernon, who was concerned over security issues. Vernon and his own mother, Minnie Mae, are also buried here, and a small plaque honors Elvis's twin brother, Jesse Garon.

The same year that the Meditation Garden was constructed, 1966, Elvis gave his girlfriend, Priscilla, a horse named Domino as a surprise gift, which fueled an equine buying spree that would result in him owning an altogether different type of property. Following the purchase of Domino, Elvis bought a horse for Sandy, the wife of his aide Jerry Schilling, so that Priscilla would have someone to ride with. Then he bought a horse for himself named Rising Sun, converted the old barn at the back of Graceland into a stable and called it "House of the Rising Sun," and, in true Elvis fashion, bought horses, saddles, and Western outfits for his entire entourage. Graceland didn't really have the room to accommodate all the horses, yet even that was no deterrent. After all, when

For Elvis, Graceland was much more than just a place to live: It was the one place where he could be himself without a media frenzy.

Elvis wanted to do something, nothing could stop him.

One day in February 1967, after yet another horse-buying expedition, he and Priscilla were driving through the Mississippi countryside about ten miles south of Graceland. They came upon a huge white cross and artificial lake overlooking a beautiful 163-acre cattle ranch. The place was named Twinkletown Farms, and for the young couple it was love at first sight. When they subsequently learned the ranch was for sale, it was a no-brainer: Within days, Elvis had signed to buy the property, cattle included, for a staggering $437,000. But the spending didn't stop there— far from it. During the next few weeks he also splashed out on more than two dozen pickup trucks for his friends, in addition to trailer homes, tractors, horse vans, hired help, wood fencing, and assorted other paraphernalia that ran up a bill in excess of $100,000.

Bored with the routine of making movies and soundtrack albums, Elvis had the time of his life on his new ranch. During this time period, Elvis was also under pressure from Priscilla's parents to marry their daughter. The Circle G Ranch, as he renamed it (after Graceland), can be seen as his final expression of bachelorhood. He loved spending his days and nights in the great outdoors, riding horses, herding cattle, holding skeet-shooting contests, hunting for turtles and snakes, partaking in picnics, and generally living out the rancher lifestyle in a communal atmosphere. In fact, Elvis enjoyed the sharing so much that he intended to give each of his friends an acre of land, but money-conscious Vernon somehow managed to talk him out of that. (Eventually, Elvis's manager, Colonel Tom Parker, managed to talk him out of the ranch as well.)

The fact was, given the recent downturn in his record sales and the low box-office receipts for his movies, Elvis was spending money faster than he was earning it. And besides, after about six months of acting out his cowboy fantasies, he began to grow tired of the Circle G. Bit by bit, things were sold off: the trailers, the tractors, the pickups, even the cattle, culminating in a public auction on November 4, 1967, that raised $108,000. This was a small amount compared to what Elvis's ranching venture had cost him, but he'd had his fun and that was what counted. A couple of years later, he sold the Circle G Ranch itself.

The classical beauty of Graceland can be seen from the first glimpse of the white columns that flank the front door.

Shortly after the Circle G auction, Elvis and Priscilla spent around $400,000 in the Trousdale Estates section of Beverly Hills on their first home in Los Angeles: a house at 1174 Hillcrest Road. Prior to this, Elvis stayed in hotels such as the Knickerbocker and Beverly Wilshire whenever he needed to spend time on the West Coast. (From 1960 to 1965, he intermittently leased the former house of the Shah of Iran at 565 Perugia Way, in the exclusive Bel Air section of Beverly Hills, and also resided at nearby 1059 Bellagio Road

A Gathering of Rock 'n' Roll Royalty

At 10:00 on the night of Friday, August 27, 1965, Elvis played host to some extra-special guests at his rented Perugia Way home in Bel Air: The Beatles. Arranged by Colonel Tom Parker, with the cooperation of Fab Four manager Brian Epstein, the meeting took place amid elaborate security arrangements. As fans gathered outside the front gates, Elvis's entourage waited anxiously inside. Only Elvis appeared cool about the whole thing, sitting in the den and watching a soundless TV when John, Paul, George, and Ringo arrived. After introducing them to Priscilla and the gang, the King played bass to Charlie Rich's "Mohair Sam," which was in repeat mode on his jukebox. Thereafter, The Beatles began mingling with some of the other guests, and John and Paul even picked up some guitars and jammed a little with Elvis, but overall the much-anticipated evening was anticlimactic.

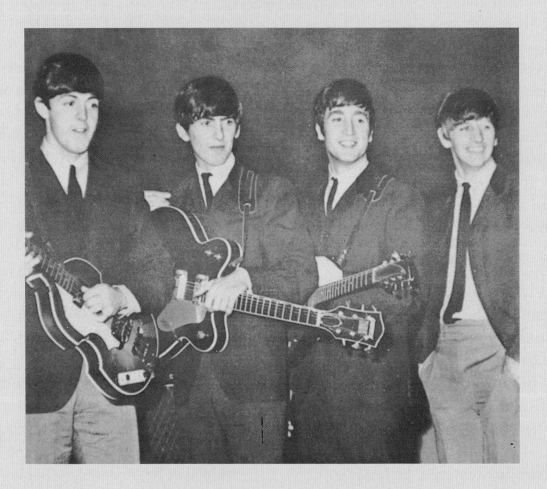

Elvis often stayed at the Beverly Wilshire Hotel while filming his early movies in Hollywood. Later, he lived in rented or purchased homes.

while making movies in 1961 and 1962.)

The last home that Elvis leased before buying the Hillcrest Road property was a ranch house at 10550 Rocca Place in Bel Air, owned by the same person who had rented him the home on Bellagio Road. Up to this point, all of his West Coast residences had served as luxurious bachelor pads, where Elvis could hang out with his cronies and play host to the

leading ladies in most of his movies. That all changed once he married Priscilla…for a time, at least. The Hillcrest home had only four bedrooms, so there wasn't enough space to accommodate Elvis's entire entourage. Within a couple of years, Elvis and Priscilla bought a much larger house at 144 Monovale Drive in Holmby Hills, affording far more room for everyone. Priscilla lived here after she and Elvis separated.

In addition to being popular with tourists, the Music Gates at Graceland are a common meeting place for fans who wish to pay tribute to the King.

The only other West Coast retreats in which Elvis invested were those in the desert resort of Palm Springs, which the Colonel introduced him to. Elvis and Priscilla spent their wedding night in a 5,000-square-foot house at 1350 Ladera Circle. The couple rented a home on Camino del Norte the following year, then purchased a 15-room house at 845 Chino Canyon Road for just under $100,000 in 1970. Elvis sometimes flew here to spend the night after performing in Las Vegas.

For all the glitz and glamour of his Beverly Hills and Palm Springs residences, not to mention the outdoor splendor of his Circle G Ranch, the only place that Elvis truly thought of as home was Graceland. It was his refuge from public life; the one place he could feel comfortable simply being himself. Toward the end of his life, peering through a window at the fans who stood in front of the music gates, Elvis reportedly confided to his nurse, Marian Cocke, that he doubted anyone would be interested in him after he died. His theory has been disproven many times over. Today, decades after his death, Graceland remains. It serves as a shrine to fans who come to get a glimpse into the private life of Elvis. Each year, on the anniversary of his death, thousands of fans gather for a week of mourning and remembrance of this legendary man.

Each year, on the evening of August 15th, fans gather in front of the Music Gate to pay tribute by singing Elvis's songs and telling stories of his life. At 11:00 P.M., two or more Graceland employees walk down to the gate with a torch that has been lighted from the eternal flame that burns at the head of Elvis's grave. Fans form a procession and reverently climb up the hill behind the house to pass single file along the grave site. This touching tribute proves that, despite Elvis's fears to the contrary, his fans are as faithful after his death as they were during his lifetime.

Perhaps the most personal and lasting tribute to Elvis is the bronze plaque that marks his final resting place. The plaque, which includes the names of his parents and daughter, Lisa Marie, bears a touching epitaph written by Vernon Presley for his son. The inscription pays tribute to Elvis's talent and professional achievements, but ends on a very per-

After Elvis's death, his uncle Vester (who was also the gatekeeper at Graceland) was inundated with requests from fans to take their cameras onto the estate and snap a picture of the mansion.

sonal note: "We miss you, Son and Daddy. I thank God that he gave us you as our son."

Soldier Boy

Fans and critics alike wondered if Elvis's career was coming to an end when he began military service. Yet it wasn't all worry and no play for US 53 310 761.

Anita Wood made frequent visits to Fort Hood, Texas, while Elvis was undergoing basic training.

On the night of Sunday, March 23, 1958, Elvis was riding the crest of a wave of popularity: Chart-topping records, hit movies, sold-out concerts, fan hysteria, and near-constant controversy all helped him become the biggest star on the planet. Yet on that March night, at the pinnacle of his success, with the world at his feet and an omnipresent support system of fans, relatives, and friends, it seemed as if he was giving it all away.

For more than a year the specter of military service hung over his head. When Uncle Sam came calling, Elvis passed his pre-induction physical and considered his options. Instead of taking the easy route chosen by so many celebrities in his

Elvis takes a bus bound for Kennedy Veterans Hospital in Memphis, where he and 12 other Army recruits were examined and processed.

position—entering Special Services to entertain the troops—he decided to show his allegiance to the Stars and Stripes by serving his time as a regular soldier. In the face of overexposure and negative publicity about his destabilizing influence on American youth, Elvis's refusal to accept special consideration was viewed by the public in an admirable light. Though he made the most of his last night as a civilian, he seemed understandably upset about leaving his loved ones and giving up the good life. And, while making positive comments to press reporters, he was also said to be privately concerned that, after two years away, he'd never be able to pick up where he left off.

On the morning of March 24, accompanied by his parents, girlfriend Anita Wood, and various friends, Elvis reported to the draft board in the M&M Building on South Main Street in Memphis, and was soon traveling on a bus toward the Kennedy Veterans Hospital, where he and twelve other recruits were examined and processed. Pronounced fit, Private Elvis Presley US 53 310 761 bid farewell to his distraught mother, weeping father, and

Anita, and boarded yet another bus, this one bound for Fort Chaffee, Arkansas. Several hundred fans were in tow, as well as a posse of reporters and photographers intent on recording his every word and action, from folding his civilian clothes to making his army bed.

The next day, after undergoing further processing procedures, the King of Rock 'n' Roll was given the most famous haircut since Samson was tricked by Delilah. Before popping flashbulbs and whirring news cameras, Elvis good-naturedly submitted himself to a standard-issue GI cut...and promptly forgot to hand over the 65¢ fee out of the generous $7 partial

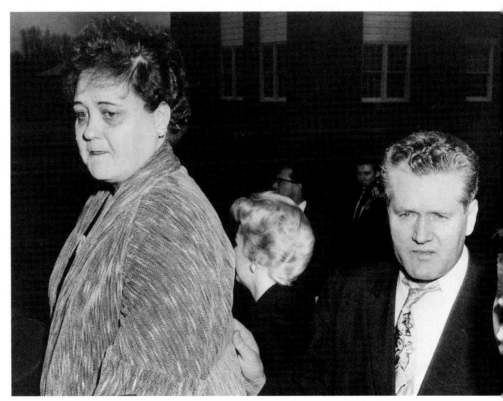

Vernon and Gladys Presley share a sad moment after watching their son board a bus bound for Fort Chaffee, Arkansas.

This is one of the last photos of Elvis with his mother. Gladys became ill while living off-base with Elvis in Fort Hood, returned to Memphis with acute hepatitis, and died there on August 14, 1958.

fragments of sideburn, the barber reminded Elvis that he owed some money.

Subsequently issued his U.S. Army uniform, Private Presley was assigned to the 2nd Armored Division at Fort Hood, Texas, for basic training and advanced tank instruction. Fans and members of the media followed him all the way there before Elvis's military superiors declared him off-limits to reporters and photographers following his first 24 hours at Fort Hood. Once the immediate attention subsided, Elvis adapted to life with his fellow recruits, though he seemed desperately homesick at times. He phoned Gladys at least once a day, and many times both of them were in tears, with Gladys begging him to take proper care of himself and Elvis trying to reassure his worried mother.

pay that he'd been given a short time earlier. While a porter used a broom to sweep up the famous locks and discarded

While some of the soldiers gave him a hard time about his celebrity status, Elvis soon became friends with others such as Privates Rex Mansfield and William Norvell, as well as Sergeant Bill Norwood who, after suggesting that Anita Wood should

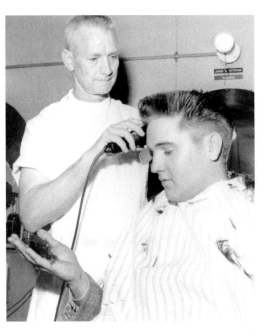

Left: *In front of the world's cameras, Elvis says good-bye to his famous locks and long sideburns.*

Below: *Sporting a standard-issue GI haircut and white T-shirt, the singing soldier gets a shot from a smiling Army doctor during his pre-induction physical.*

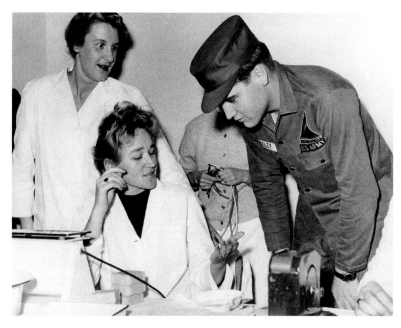

Left: *The King chats with a young nurse before donating blood for the German Red Cross in January 1959. He was one of 200 American soldiers giving blood that day at the Friedberg dispensary.*

Below: *On the morning of March 24, 1958, Elvis is sworn into the U.S. Army by an officer at the M&M Building on South Main Street in Memphis.*

A few months after joining the 1st Medium Tank Battalion, 32nd Armor, 3rd Armored Division, Elvis was promoted to Private First Class for his endeavors in field exercises.

visit, made his home available to her. Consequently, by the time he completed basic training at the end of May, the teen idol had begun to settle in. He earned his marksman's medal with a carbine and was classified as a sharpshooter with a pistol. Elvis had always loved guns, so it made perfect sense that he excelled in these exercises.

On leave for two weeks at the start of June 1958, Elvis spent time with family and friends. He also recorded several new tracks in Nashville to help satisfy RCA's need for new material while he was out of commission. Then he returned to Fort Hood, and after receiving the standard

soldier's permission to live off base with his "dependents," he obtained a three-bedroom trailer home and moved there with his parents, grandmother Minnie Mae, and friend Lamar Fike. When the trailer became a little too cramped, following the arrival of cousins Gene and Junior Smith, he simply rented a house where he could stay with his family on the weekends while undergoing advanced tank training during the week. Friends from all over would drop by, and Gladys would prepare food for everyone. All in all it was a pretty cozy setup until Gladys's health declined, and she and Vernon had to return to Memphis at the start of August.

A smiling Elvis is captured by news cameras while on night maneuvers at the Grafenwohr exercise camp in December 1958. A week later he spent part of Christmas Eve helping to decorate the company's Christmas tree.

tal on August 9 with acute hepatitis. Having completed his advanced tank training, Elvis was about to commence his basic unit training, but it quickly became clear that his mother's condition was serious. On August 12 the Army granted him emergency leave. Elvis headed straight for the hospital, and when his mother saw him she appeared to rally. However, during the early hours of Thursday, August 14, 1958, with Vernon by her side while Elvis was at home, Gladys Love Presley succumbed to a massive heart attack. She was just 46. It was a blow from which Elvis would never fully recover.

Ever since her son's induction, Gladys had been anxious about his well-being and distraught at the thought of his absence for an extended period of time. Now extremely sick and unable to eat, Gladys was admitted to Methodist Hospi-

Elvis broke down several times in the days leading up to his mother's funeral.

All Aboard!

Fans and media representatives turned out in force when Elvis was due to board ship for his military trip to Europe. So, with Colonel Parker orchestrating the proceedings, and to the strains of an Army band playing "Tutti Frutti," Elvis put on his best smile for the cameras as he walked up the gangplank of the U.S.S. *General Randall*...and walked, and walked, and walked. In total, he went through the boarding routine eight times until everyone was satisfied, and then soon afterward, while the band played a medley of his hits, the ship set sail and Elvis left the United States for the first and, as things would turn out, only time.

He sobbed hysterically while Gladys's favorite gospel group, the Blackwood Brothers, performed at the service in the Memphis Funeral Home, and he was equally inconsolable at her Forest Hill Cemetery grave site, crying out, "Oh God, everything I have is gone."

The mourning continued through the next few days as Elvis was granted extended leave. Evidently his fans were grieving too—they sent him more than 100,000 cards and letters, around 500 telegrams, and more than 200 floral arrangements to express their sympathy for his loss. Still, even though it would never be the same, life had to carry on. Elvis returned to Fort Hood on August 24, and within a month he shipped out to join the 1st Medium Tank Battalion, 32nd Armor, 3rd Armored Division in what was then known as West Germany. Along the way, Colonel Tom Parker organized a press conference when Elvis's troop train arrived in Brooklyn, New York, at which he answered questions about his army duty, his music, and his mom. He offered a heartfelt account of his continued mourning to the assembled reporters:

> Everyone loses their mother, but I was an only child, and Mother was always right with me all my life. And it wasn't only like losing a mother, it was like losing a friend, a companion, someone to talk to. I could wake her up any hour of the night if I was worried or troubled about something...she'd get up and try to help me.

During the transatlantic trip aboard the U.S.S. *General Randall,* Elvis bonded with a fellow singer named Charlie Hodge, whom he'd met on the troop train to Brooklyn, and together they took charge of a talent show. But without his mother to see or talk to ever again, Elvis seemed lonely and adrift.

In West Germany, there was another press conference and further meet-and-greets during the first few days. Vernon and his mother, Minnie Mae—whom Elvis had affectionately called "Dodger" ever since she had ducked away from a ball he had thrown at her as a child—set up residence with Elvis and his

friends Red West and Lamar Fike in a couple of hotels: one in Bad Homburg, near Frankfurt; the other in Bad Nauheim, about 20 minutes from the base. Elvis

Fatigued in his fatigues: Elvis takes time out to read some fan mail.

Change of Address

Elvis, Vernon, Minnie Mae, Red West, Lamar Fike, and Elisabeth Stefaniak occupied the top floor of the refined Hotel Grunewald in Bad Nauheim, but they quickly fell out of favor with the management and other guests thanks to the unruly behavior of the King and his courtiers. Vernon, Minnie Mae, and Elisabeth weren't the problem; it was the other three, constantly roughhousing with one another to the point where nobody could get any peace and quiet. One night at the end of January 1959 their antics went too far. Elvis, chased by Red down a hallway, locked himself in his bedroom, and Red tried to smoke him out by setting fire to a piece of paper and sliding it under his door. Before they knew it, the flames were out of control. When the manager, Herr Schmidt, learned about the incident, Elvis and company were asked to leave the hotel. The group soon found a rental house at 14 Goethestrasse (pictured), where they lived for the duration of Elvis's tour of duty.

would rise every morning at 5:30, eat the breakfast Dodger had prepared for him, and leave for base by 6:30 in a black Mercedes taxi, before returning for lunch and dinner. The only exception was Friday, when Elvis and his fellow soldiers had to stay late into the evening, cleaning the toilets and their barracks for weekly inspection the following morning. It had been a long time since the King was obliged to do any such chores, yet he mucked in with the other soldiers and did his best to be perceived— during the day, at least—as just a regular guy.

Elvis signs autographs for fans while on leave in Paris. He visited the French capital on two occasions during his time in the Army.

Some evenings, Elvis and his friends surreptitiously went to the movies— sneaking into theaters after the lights went down and leaving just before the final credits to avoid being noticed—and even to a couple of Bill Haley concerts.

Elvis also dated a few girls while keeping in regular phone contact with Anita Wood back in America. Through November and much of December, Private Presley went on maneuvers at Grafenwohr and was promoted to Private First Class for his endeavors in field exercises. It was reportedly around this time that one of the sergeants introduced him to amphetamines as a means of staying awake during the long hours of training. For Elvis, taking amphetamines quickly became a regular habit.

Although he returned to Bad Nauheim to spend the holiday season with family and friends, he also spent part of Christmas Eve helping to decorate the company's Christmas tree. Then, at the start of January 1959, one of the girls whom Elvis had briefly dated, 19-year-old Elisabeth Stefa-

Elvis poses with showgirls during a visit to the Moulin Rouge nightclub in Munich, Germany.

niak, moved into the Hotel Grunewald with him and his inner circle, having accepted an invitation to work as his secretary. It was particularly handy that, courtesy of her German mother and American stepfather, Elisabeth was bilingual. So, installing herself in a corner room at the hotel, she answered his fan mail and became romantically involved with him despite the knowledge that he continued to see other girls.

In early February the Presley clan relocated to a three-story, five-bedroom house at Goethestrasse 14, which afforded everyone more space and privacy than the nearby Hotel Grunewald. For the exorbitant rent of $800 a month, it also provided them with a landlady named Frau Pieper who doubled as their housekeeper. At last, Elvis was living in a home where he could relax away from prying eyes, listen to records, entertain friends, and sit at a piano to play and sing his favorite songs. He came home every day for lunch, and each evening he would spend time signing autographs for fans who waited patiently in front of the house. On Sundays he and some friends would play touch football just down the street.

Early in 1959, accompanied by friends Red West and Lamar Fike, Elvis used a three-day pass to visit Munich and call unannounced on Vera Tschechowa, an

A somber young Priscilla bids Elvis farewell at the Rhein-Main air base in Germany.

18-year-old actress whom he'd met a few months earlier. Together, they visited the Moulin Rouge nightclub. As usual, the press was on hand to photograph Elvis with his "latest flame." In this case they also took numerous shots of him posing with the club's showgirls, but all it really amounted to was a footloose and fancy-free young man having some fun. Enough fun, in fact, for him to pay a return visit to Munich's Moulin Rouge nightclub in mid-June before continuing his two-week furlough by traveling to Paris and dropping in on the original Moulin Rouge.

By June, Red West had returned to the United States, so Elvis was accompanied by Lamar Fike as well as his two army buddies Charlie Hodge and Rex Mansfield when visiting Parisian nightspots including the Lido, the Folies Bergère, and a club called Le Bantu that didn't even open until 4:00 A.M. All in all, the Paris stopover was reported to have been a live-by-night, sleep-by-day adventure. Elvis returned to the French capital for one last adventure in January 1960, although by then a new girl was occupying his thoughts.

Fourteen-year-old Priscilla Beaulieu had only recently been voted "Queen of Del Valley Junior High" by her classmates in Austin, Texas, when 24-year-old Elvis Presley first met her on the evening of

Fans peer through the window as Elvis and Priscilla share a moment alone on the way to the airport for his return to the United States.

Sunday, September 13, 1959. Brunette, with a sensuous mouth and sultry blue eyes, she was wearing a navy and white sailor dress with white socks and shoes; he, a bright red sweater and tan slacks. Brenda Lee's "Sweet Nothin's" was spinning on the record player.

Priscilla, as can be expected, seemed in awe of the superstar, while Elvis was said to be instantly infatuated with the beautiful stepdaughter of Air Force Captain Joseph Beaulieu. Captain Beaulieu had been transferred to Wiesbaden, a 45-minute drive from Bad Nauheim, just a month earlier, and Priscilla had been invited to visit Elvis at his home by mutual acquaintance Currie Grant, a U.S. Airman and assistant manager at Wiesbaden air force venue the Eagle Club.

Elvis spent the rest of that Sunday evening talking to Priscilla and, amid a room full of friends, even sang to her. It wasn't long before he asked Currie Grant to invite her back.

Soon Elvis and Priscilla began dating, and after Elvis met Priscilla's parents and convinced them that his intentions were honorable, they saw each other frequently during his last few months in

Elvis meets the press on March 3, 1960, just two days before his discharge from the U.S. Army. He answered questions on several topics, including his relationship with 14-year-old Priscilla Beaulieu.

surprisingly little publicity about his interest in Priscilla.

Elvis was promoted to sergeant on January 20, 1960, received his stripes on February 11, and was scheduled to be discharged from the Army in early March. Accordingly, he began preparing for the resumption of his life at Graceland and his career in Nashville and Hollywood, sending old girlfriend Anita Wood a French poodle for Christmas and calling her more frequently as his return to America drew closer.

West Germany. Because of Elvis's inability to go out in public unrecognized (and without creating a mob scene), most of his dates with Priscilla consisted of her visits to his house, where they were surrounded by Elvis's family members and friends. Although a relationship with someone so young could have had a ruinous effect on Elvis's image, there was

Regardless, word of his relationship with Priscilla did reach the media, and on March 2, the day of his departure from West Germany, press photographers and news cameras captured her somber face as she waved good-bye to her love at the Rhein-Main airbase. The photos ended up in *Life* magazine, and Priscilla was labeled "the

Sergeant Presley was greeted by Frank Sinatra's 19-year-old daughter, Nancy, after disembarking in Fort Dix, New Jersey, just prior to his discharge from the Army.

girl he left behind." Which she was...for the time being.

Discharged on Saturday, March 5, after disembarking in Fort Dix, New Jersey, Elvis finally arrived back in Memphis two days later amid a snowstorm and much hoopla. That afternoon, sitting in his father's office behind the main house at Graceland, he gave a press conference, during which he acknowledged—yet tried to play down—his relationship with Priscilla Beaulieu, focusing instead on how happy he was to be back home. "I just can't get it in my mind that I'm here," he told the media.

Elvis wasn't the only Presley to find a new love in Germany. His father, Vernon, met Dee Stanley while the Presley family was living in Bad Nauheim. At the time they met, Dee was in the process of divorcing her military husband. Dee returned to America with Vernon after Elvis's discharge, and the two were married in Huntsville, Alabama, in July 1960. Elvis did not attend his father's wedding, which led to speculation that the marriage caused friction between the two men. (Elvis not only gained a stepmother, but he got three stepbrothers as well.)

As time would tell, Elvis was a changed man when he emerged from the Army. Critics speculated that the damage done to his career during his two years in the Army could be irreparable. Instead, Elvis surprised everyone by trading in the frenzied trappings of his rock 'n' roll youth for a more mature image built on the good publicity from his tour of duty. The success of his movies and pop music albums was a testament to the wide appeal of his new, more mellow style.

The King's Courtiers

With his unbeatable combination of talent, fame, wealth, power, and incredible personal charm, Elvis was never short of company or people willing to please him.

Having grown up somewhat of a loner, content in the company of his parents and his own inner thoughts, the adult Elvis countered spiritual isolation and personal insecurities with the constant presence of family and friends. There were times when he sought privacy, either to contemplate or meditate, but for the vast majority of his waking hours, and even those when he was asleep, he didn't want to be alone. He surrounded himself with an around-the-clock entourage of male helpers and recreational chums, and courted a steady stream of women to satisfy his need for passion and companionship.

Because he achieved a certain measure of fame before he was out of his teens, and then superstardom during his early twenties, for his entire adult life Elvis had people on hand to indulge his every whim, and see to his every desire. For that reason his concept of a male-female relationship was said to be strictly one-sided: The woman had to remain absolutely faithful and display no interest whatsoever in other men, whereas he was free to do as he pleased. The women in Elvis's life had to tolerate his behavior, turn a blind eye to it, or end the relationship and move on.

Despite his lack of fidelity, Elvis was a prize catch: He was a handsome, warm, witty, affectionate, kind, courteous, thoughtful, fun-loving, and generous man who, despite his occasional flashes of temper, could be a terrific friend. Indeed, many of the attributes that characterized his dynamic, charismatic public persona were part of the private Elvis, too. It's not too surprising that so many women found his charms impossible to resist.

Though he dated a few different girls while in high school—including Betty McMahan, Billie Wardlaw, and Regis Vaughan—Elvis's first serious girlfriend was Dixie Locke, who captured his atten-

Throughout his life, Elvis loved celebrating the Christmas season with family and friends. In this 1957 photo, Elvis shows off a few of his holiday gifts.

15-year-old sophomore at South Side High who seemed instantly fascinated by the combination of Elvis's shyness and his outrageous appearance. At one church event, Dixie made a point of loudly telling a friend that she planned to go roller-skating at the Rainbow Roller-dome the following Saturday. Elvis took the bait and turned up in a short black bullfighter's jacket, black pegged pants with a pink stripe down the legs, and a ruffled shirt. Not exactly conventional skating attire—but then, he couldn't skate anyway. He was only there for one reason, and this time it was Dixie who took the bait, introducing herself to Elvis and initiating a conversation that continued right through the evening.

It was a mutual attraction, and after going to a movie the very next night, they became a hot item, seeing each other almost every day for the next several months while pursuing the typical 1950s American teen lifestyle: watching movies and taking walks in the park; having milk shakes and meals at the drive-in; watching television and listening to records on nights when their parents weren't home;

tion at the Assembly of God Church in South Memphis in early 1954. He was a 19-year-old hipster with long sideburns, slicked-back hair, and flamboyant clothes; she was a pretty, dark-haired, cruising around town in the car and listening to the radio; and, perhaps not as commonplace, attending church, disc jockey Bob Neal's *High Noon Round-Up* radio show at the WMPS studio, and all-night gospel singing sessions at the Ellis Auditorium.

Early in the summer of 1954, Elvis quit his job at Precision Tool to drive a truck for Crown Electric, and he and Dixie were already contemplating marriage. In fact, there was one occasion when they very nearly eloped, before apparently thinking better of it since Dixie was still in high school. Meanwhile, Elvis was making cursory attempts to launch a singing career, and while Dixie was on a two-week family vacation at the start of July, he recorded his first single and B-side for Sun Records, "That's All Right"/"Blue Moon of Kentucky." By the time she returned home, both songs were all over the local radio airwaves.

Dixie remained true to Elvis while he performed in venues around town and on the radio, but as his career took off he spent more and more time on the road, and he quickly settled into a pattern of playing the field while demanding that his partner stay at home and not even socialize. Dixie was the first of many to grow tired of this arrangement—she and Elvis ended their relationship in the summer of 1955.

Amid a succession of brief encounters, the next steady dates for "the Nation's Only Atomic-Powered Singer" were 18-year-old June Juanico and 19-year-old Barbara Hearn... simultaneously. Elvis met June at a performance in her hometown of Biloxi, Mississippi, and embarked on a full-blown relationship with her about a year later, in the summer of 1956. They began seeing each other when June paid a visit to Memphis, and then Elvis returned the compliment by taking a three-week Gulf Coast vacation in Biloxi. It wasn't long before the local press was buzzing with rumors that Elvis and June were engaged.

Fun-loving and more than capable of standing up for herself, June earned Elvis's respect while proving herself to be his equal in terms of stubbornness and determination. When Elvis's visit ended, she accompanied him on a concert tour of Florida. Then he left for Hollywood to make his first movie, *Love Me Tender,* and pursued assorted starlets and actresses, including Debra Paget and Natalie Wood. That September, toward the end of filming, Elvis took a few days off to fulfill a return engagement at the Mississippi–Alabama Fair and Dairy Show in Tupelo, where he gave his first public performance at age ten. Escorting him there were Vernon and Gladys, as well his "Memphis girlfriend," Barbara Hearn, whom Elvis continued to see right

Elvis enjoyed a relationship with 18-year-old June Juanico in 1956; here, the two share their love of horseback riding.

up until June Juanico arrived in Memphis for a week-long visit on October 19.

Things must have been getting very confusing—if not for Elvis, then certainly for Vernon and Gladys, who had bonded with both girls, and also for the less-than-eagle-eyed local media. When

Elvis's car was vandalized outside a Memphis movie theater, a newspaper report mistakenly named Barbara Hearn as his date when it should have been June Juanico. Elvis, meanwhile, was clearly capable of juggling several balls at the same time—after Natalie Wood spent a few days with him in Memphis,

Natalie Wood's visit to Memphis during the fall of 1956 was closely chronicled by the local press, who couldn't resist the story of a hometown boy showing a big star around town.

When June Juanico spotted newspaper photos of Elvis and Dottie Harmony exchanging Christmas gifts, she apparently decided enough was enough and ended her relationship with Elvis. Not long afterward, she fell in love with a more committed man and accepted his proposal of marriage. Dottie, meanwhile, didn't return to California until January 4, 1957, when Elvis left for New York to

he dated nightclub dancers Marilyn Evans and Dottie Harmony during a Las Vegas vacation in early November. Both women visited Elvis in Memphis the following month—Marilyn in early December, Dottie in time for Christmas. Both women met Vernon and Gladys Presley, and were seen—and photographed—all over town with Elvis.

June Juanico, seen here in a tender moment with Elvis, later chronicled their romance in her 1997 book Elvis: In the Twilight of Memory.

Yvonne Lime, who had a small role in Elvis's second movie, Loving You, *was one of many starlets he dated early in his Hollywood career. Yvonne joined Elvis and his parents at Graceland for Easter weekend, 1957. Here, Elvis and Yvonne are pictured posing in his car during a date.*

While dating June Juanico, Elvis also spent plenty of time with 19-year-old Barbara Hearn, seen here watching Elvis play the piano in the Presley house on Audubon Drive in 1956.

mid-January 1957 to begin work on his second film, *Loving You,* and he soon turned his attention toward a number of pretty starlets, including Yvonne Lime, who had a small role in the movie. Yvonne was the first in a series of movie costars and crew members that Elvis dated.

The more notable costars whom Elvis was involved with included Juliet Prowse (*G.I. Blues,* 1960),

Elvis never dated the love interest in his first movie, Love Me Tender, *but it wasn't for lack of trying. Debra Paget, seen here on the set of* The Loves of Omar Khayam, *consistently rejected the young heart-throb's advances, so he quickly turned his attention in a number of other directions.*

appear on *The Ed Sullivan Show,* where he wore a gold lamé vest that was a Christmas present from Barbara Hearn. (If you are having trouble keeping up with all of this, you're not the only one.)

As Elvis's manager, Colonel Parker was said to be unhappy when any one girl was too closely associated with his boy—having him seem "unavailable" was bad for business. It's not clear just how much this influenced Elvis, but before long he ended his relationships with Dottie and Barbara. Elvis arrived in Hollywood in

Judy Tyler

Among the leading ladies Elvis *didn't* date was Judy Tyler, who portrayed Peggy Van Alden, his girlfriend and manager in *Jailhouse Rock*. Recently married to actor Gregory Lafayette, Judy had played Princess Summerfall Winterspring on the children's television program *Howdy Doody* and taken to the Broadway stage in the Rodgers and Hammerstein musical *Pipe Dreams*. On July 3, 1957, just three weeks after *Jailhouse Rock* completed filming, Judy and Gregory were killed in a car accident near Billy the Kid, Wyoming. "She was at the peak of success," a distraught Elvis was reported saying in the next day's *Memphis Commercial Appeal*. "Nothing has hurt

me as bad in my life.... All of us boys really loved that girl. She meant a lot to all of us. I don't believe I can stand to see the movie we made together now, just don't believe I can." Although he wanted to attend the funeral even if it meant missing the premiere of *Loving You*, Elvis sent flowers instead to avoid disrupting the service.

Colonel Tom Parker

In the Elvis legend, the Colonel is often portrayed as the villain—a sinister, underhanded force who controlled the singer's every move and influenced his every decision. Those who see him in this light point to his background as a carnival huckster, his unsophisticated approach to promotion, and the questionable movie deals Elvis became locked into during the 1960s as proof of Parker's notorious character. In the early 1980s, information came to light that bolstered this negative depiction of the Colonel. During the course of a lawsuit filed against Parker by Elvis's estate, which stemmed from a court-ordered investigation of Parker's management of Elvis, the Colonel admitted that he was not Thomas Parker from Huntington, West Virginia, but Andreas van Kuijk from Breda, Holland. This information had surfaced earlier, but Parker did not admit his true identity until it was to his advantage to do so. He used the information to declare that he was not an American citizen, and therefore he could not be sued under federal laws. The case was later settled out of court. Parker died in 1997 after suffering a stroke.

Former carnival huckster and honorary colonel, Tom Parker turned Elvis into a multimillionaire and a household name after taking over the managerial reins in 1955. However, he generally stayed out of his client's personal affairs.

with Nancy Sinatra was rumored to have heated up.

Other actresses whom Elvis dated during his career in Hollywood included Joan Blackman while working on *Kid Galahad* (1962), Yvonne Craig while shooting *It Happened at the World's Fair* (1963), Mary Ann Mobley while working on *Girl Happy* (1965), and Deborah Walley during the production of *Spinout* (1966).

Perhaps his most serious involvement with a costar was his relationship with Ann-Margret, which began during production of *Viva Las Vegas* in 1963, at a time when Priscilla Beaulieu was his live-in girlfriend at Graceland. A beautiful, red-haired actress, singer, and dancer who'd just scored a major hit starring in the film version of the Broadway musical *Bye Bye Birdie*, 22-year-old Ann-Margret had the talent and the dynamic personality to earn her equal billing with Elvis Presley, something that very few of his other costars achieved. It seemed clear from the start of filming that they were well suited in other ways, too, both on and off the set, and by the time filming switched from the Vegas

The natural chemistry between Elvis and Ann-Margret created sparks both on and off the screen, resulting in a hit movie and a serious romance.

Tuesday Weld (*Wild in the Country,* 1961), Stella Stevens (*Girls! Girls! Girls!,* 1962), and Ann-Margret (*Viva Las Vegas,* 1964). Elvis was also rumored to have been involved with Nancy Sinatra, his costar in *Speedway* (1968). Juliet Prowse was actually engaged to Nancy Sinatra's father, Frank, when she and Elvis became romantically involved. And Elvis was married to Priscilla when his relationship

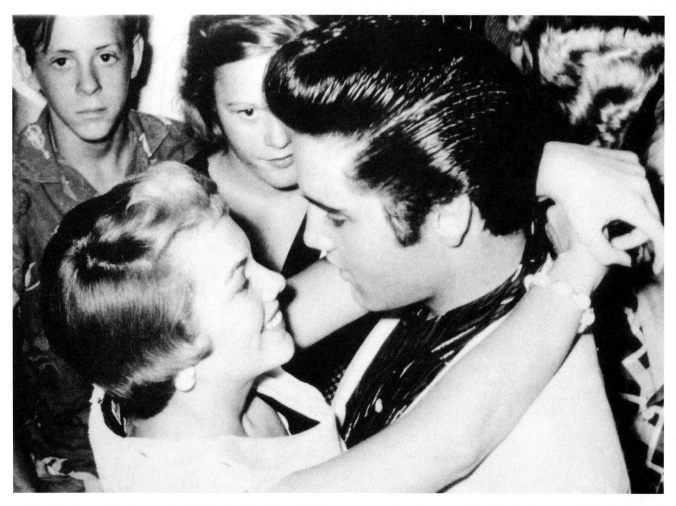

Anita Wood was Elvis's steady girlfriend throughout the late 1950s and early '60s. "Little bittie," as Elvis liked to call her, often turned a blind eye to her boyfriend's philandering, but she called it quits once it became clear that Elvis was serious about Priscilla Beaulieu.

location to the Hollywood soundstage, the pair seemed virtually inseparable.

In many ways, Ann-Margret was a mirror image of Elvis: She was sexy, funny, exciting, full of energy, and enjoyed the same kind of music. She even shared his passion for riding Harley-Davidsons. She got along well with members of Elvis's entourage, who gave her the nicknames "Rusty Ammo" and "Ann-Margrock."

Though Elvis was already committed to Priscilla, those around him were quick to remark on his deep connection to Ann-Margret. No one had ever seen him so happy, so at ease around a female companion, and soon the newspapers were full of reports about their romance. When Priscilla read the stories, she reportedly tried to visit the set, but Elvis managed to keep her at bay. When he returned to Graceland after filming, he maintained constant, if covert, phone contact with Ann-Margret.

The two resumed their relationship when Elvis returned to the West Coast in October 1963 for his next picture, *Kissin' Cousins.* The next month, ignoring Elvis's best efforts to keep her at home, Priscilla flew out to discover precisely what was going on. And when papers everywhere ran an interview in which Ann-Margret disclosed to a British reporter that she and Elvis were going steady and that she was in love, Priscilla knew all the rumors were true. Elvis reportedly mollified Priscilla by assuring her that she was the only girl for him and that he could never settle down with someone as career-minded as himself. He assured her that the affair was over, but when Priscilla returned to Memphis, Elvis resumed his relationship with Ann-Margret as soon as she returned from London, where she'd attended the royal premiere of *Bye Bye Birdie.* Although Elvis seemed to believe Ann-Margret's assertion that the British press had misquoted her, their relationship cooled, and by early 1964 it had fizzled completely. Though the relationship did not work out, the pair remained friends for the rest of Elvis's life.

The Ann-Margret episode was by no means the first time Priscilla had cause for concern, and it definitely wasn't the last. For her, the cycle of suspicion began

as soon as Elvis returned to America following his stint in the Army. At that time, his steady girlfriend was still Anita Wood, whom he'd been dating since mid-1957, shortly after he completed work on *Jailhouse Rock.* Nineteen years old when she first met Elvis, Anita was a pretty blond singer and beauty contest winner with ambitions to become an actress. Elvis saw her appearance on Wink Martindale's Memphis television show, *Top Ten Dance Party,* and it wasn't long before she was given a tour of Graceland, introduced to Elvis's parents, and given a "friendship ring" comprising a diamond surrounded by 18 sapphires.

Anita consistently believed Elvis when he denied rumors about, or evidence of, his involvement with other women. The same held true once Priscilla entered his life—at that point, Elvis's twin loves experienced twin paranoia: Anita in Memphis, concerned about the girl in Germany; and Priscilla in Germany, fretting over the singer/actress in Memphis. In both cases, their boyfriend's charm won them over. However, in the summer of 1962, once Anita learned that Priscilla was staying with Elvis in Los Angeles, it seemed clear that they'd never get married, so she ended the relationship and moved on.

In July 1972, following his marriage to and separation from Priscilla, Elvis met the next big love of his life. Blond, 22-year-old Linda Thompson was the reigning Miss Tennessee. She was fun, easygoing, straightforward, affectionate, and as time would tell during the most difficult period of his life, extremely loyal. It didn't take long for Linda to discover that Elvis had an addiction to prescription drugs, but she adjusted to his moods, his faltering health, and his nocturnal exis- tence—he often stayed up all night and slept through the day. But after four years amid the most trying of circumstances, Linda eventually found it impossible to cope with Elvis's lifestyle and ended their relationship in 1976.

By this time, he had fallen for 20-year-old Ginger Alden, the reigning Miss Mid-South, whose sister, Terry, was the reigning Miss Tennessee. Elvis was more than twice her age, and seemed perplexed by Ginger, who often appeared less interested in being around him than away from him. The more she played hard to get—supposedly refusing to accompany him on concert tours and sneaking out of the house after he fell asleep—the more he tried to keep her close, even proposing marriage with an engagement ring featur- ing an 11½-carat diamond taken from

one of his own rings. Their relationship staggered on, and Ginger was still with Elvis when he passed away on August 16, 1977. Indeed, she was the last person to see him alive, and discovered his lifeless body on the bathroom floor at Graceland.

When Ginger raised the alarm, the first two people on the scene were Al Strada and Joe Esposito, who tried in vain to resuscitate their friend and employer. While Al was Elvis's valet, Joe had long been the leader of a group known as the Memphis Mafia, a select inner circle of handlers, bodyguards, and friends who

Elvis enjoyed a few days in Hawaii in 1977 with his girlfriend, 20-year-old Memphis beauty queen Ginger Alden.

catered to Elvis's every need, whether it was keeping him company, finding him women, providing his medication, arranging his daily activities, or fulfilling his most outlandish requests.

At the start of his career, Elvis was accompanied on the road only by his cousins Gene and Junior Smith. As the King's celebrity grew, so did his needs and demands, along with the financial clout to ensure that almost any situation could be expedited. Accordingly, Elvis surrounded himself with people who could be relied on to fulfill his wishes, and who in turn relied on him for financial support.

Elvis surrounded himself with many longtime associates, including Humes High School classmate and WHBQ disc jockey George Klein; Humes classmate and bodyguard Red West, who also composed a few of his employer's songs; Red's cousin, bodyguard Sonny West; hairstylist and spiritual mentor Larry Geller; on-call doctor George Nichopolous, who prescribed most of Elvis's medications; and all-around helpers Joe Esposito, Charlie Hodge, Lamar Fike, Alan Fortas, Marty Lacker, and Jerry Schilling, along with Elvis's cousin Billy Smith and stepbrothers Rick, Billy, and David Stanley. Others came and went, and several of the men also popped up in Elvis's movies, occasionally speaking a line, but more often on the receiving end of his karate kicks and punches in the obligatory fight scenes.

Colonel Tom Parker invariably attended to all career and financial matters— adhering to the "Taking Care of Business" credo that Elvis imparted to all his

The Memphis Mafia

Black mohair suits, black hats, and dark glasses were often the uniform for Elvis and his sidekicks when they wanted to look sharp in public during the early '60s, and it was this image that helped earn the King's cronies their nickname. Once, while staying at the Sahara Hotel during a trip to Las Vegas, Elvis and his friends had an afternoon appointment at the Riviera. When they arrived, a crowd of people watched them climb out of two black limos, and their all-black visage prompted one person to yell, "Who are they? The Mafia?" A local newspaper reporter heard this, and in a story that ran the next day she referred to the group as the "Memphis Mafia." The name stuck, as did the image, although the traditional code of silence was broken just before their self-appointed "Godfather's" death when three of Elvis's former bodyguards—Red West, Sonny West, and Dave Hebler—gave interviews for a tell-all book titled *Elvis: What Happened?*

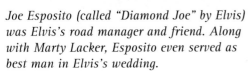

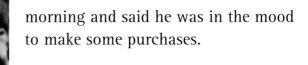

morning and said he was in the mood to make some purchases.

And it was worth it—one night in July 1975, after Elvis had argued with most of his band members, his way of apologizing was to buy them each a piece of jewelry. Since Hays didn't have enough in his case to satisfy demand,

Joe Esposito (called "Diamond Joe" by Elvis) was Elvis's road manager and friend. Along with Marty Lacker, Esposito even served as best man in Elvis's wedding.

helpers, which manifested itself in the "TCB" ("Taking Care of Business") logo that adorned everything from jewelry to backstage passes. Others were rewarded handsomely for offering their services at any time of the night and day (usually the night, given Elvis's sleeping habits) including a dentist; a car dealer; even a jeweler, Lowell Hays. Hays accompanied Elvis on tour and was always ready with a case full of jewelry for the occasions when the King called his hotel room in the wee hours of the

Elvis gave bodyguard Alan Fortas the nickname "Hog Ears." During the 1960s Fortas served as the custodian of the Circle G Ranch.

Longtime friend and Memphis Mafia member Sonny West (pictured) gave accounts of Elvis's private life to author Steve Dunleavy, who used them in his book Elvis: What Happened?

he had his brother bring more jewelry in a private plane from Memphis to Asheville, North Carolina, where the next concert was scheduled to take place. In just a few hours, Elvis spent $137,616, but he was happy. So, no doubt, were the band members and the jeweler.

As Priscilla Beaulieu Presley concluded in her autobiography, *Elvis and Me:* "I don't think anyone can begin to capture the magic, sensitivity, vulnerability, charm, generosity, and greatness of this man."

✧   ✧   ✧

Vernon Presley's second wife, Dee, had three sons: Billy, David, and Rick. Dee and the Stanley brothers coauthored the 1979 book Elvis, We Love You Tender.

Faith and Marriage

Priscilla's move to Graceland was like a fairy tale come true, yet she also had to compete with Elvis's growing quest for spiritual enlightenment.

After Elvis was discharged from the Army, his only contact with Priscilla Beaulieu was over the phone and by mail. Two months shy of her 15th birthday, the blue-eyed brunette with the turned-up nose remained in Germany when Elvis departed for the United States. Within days there were reports that he was dating Nancy Sinatra. It was three weeks before Priscilla next heard his voice, reassuring her that she was the only girl for him, and over the next two years she grew accustomed to the rumors and his denials, as well as the pain and frustration that came with loving the world's biggest heartthrob from a distance of several thousand miles.

In a press conference on the day he arrived back at Graceland, Elvis played down his relationship with "the girl he left behind." But in truth, though he was dating Anita Wood and several actresses, he seemed to have reserved a special place in his heart for "Cilla." For the time being, Elvis went along with the Colonel's belief that an all-consuming relationship would hurt his image and be bad for his career. Priscilla patiently waited for their reunion.

During their conversations, Elvis would discuss his career, even his relationship with Anita Wood, causing Priscilla to wonder where she fit in. However, he also insisted that he wanted her to visit Graceland. Cilla just had to hang on. And she did for nearly two years, even amid newspaper and magazine articles linking Elvis to beauties such as Juliet Prowse and Tuesday Weld. Then, one day in March 1962, after several months without contact, Elvis called Priscilla out of the blue and invited her to join him in Los Angeles. Simultaneously stunned and overjoyed, she pointed out that, although her mother might be receptive to this idea, it would be nearly impossible to persuade her father, Captain Paul Beaulieu. It was a challenge Elvis seemed happy to accept.

After nearly eight years together, Priscilla Beaulieu and Elvis Presley were married in a double-ring ceremony at the Aladdin Hotel in Las Vegas on May 1, 1967. Although many of the memoirs by Elvis's former friends and bodyguards suggest that Elvis was not comfortable with marriage, others recalled that Elvis was content and happy, even ecstatic at times.

While Priscilla prevailed upon her mother, Elvis spoke with the Captain several times and finally won him over by agreeing to a list of rules: the two-week-long vacation wouldn't take place until Priscilla was out of school for the summer; Elvis would send her a first-class round-trip ticket; the Beaulieus would be provided with a comprehensive itinerary of her daily activities in Los Angeles; she would be chaperoned everywhere; she'd write to her parents every day; and at night she'd stay with his friends, George and Shirley Barris. Which is what happened . . . for the most part.

Priscilla arrived in Los Angeles in June, and following a visit to Elvis's house on

Bellagio Road, she did stay at the Barris home—for one night. The next afternoon, Elvis informed her that he had planned a trip to Las Vegas, and shortly after midnight she was sitting next to him in his luxury motor home on the way to Nevada. She slyly circumvented the problem of her parents receiving letters each day by quickly pre-writing a week's worth and asking Elvis's butler to mail them from Los Angeles. Their next stop was the Sahara Hotel and Casino, where the King and his princess shared a suite.

During twelve blissful, fun-filled days and nights in Las Vegas, Elvis took Priscilla shopping, chose the clothes she should wear, and instructed her on how to style her hair and apply heavier makeup. Elvis liked his women to wear plenty of eyeliner and mascara, and Priscilla readily accepted his choices. Courtesy of a hairdresser at the hotel, her tresses were teased and twisted into a beehive style, her eyes were heavily made up, and the result was the apparent transformation of an innocent teen into a sophisticated siren.

After her return to Germany, Priscilla had something to look forward to during the next six months: Christmas at Graceland. Elvis had invited her, and once again she had to persuade her parents. However, that request was nothing compared to what the Beaulieus were confronted with once the Christmas trip was over and their darling daughter returned home: Elvis wanted her to finish school in Memphis.

Elvis called Captain Beaulieu and used all his powers of persuasion. If Cilla moved to Memphis, he promised, she wouldn't live with him at Graceland but with Vernon and his wife in their house nearby. She would be enrolled in the very best Catholic school, where he'd ensure that she would graduate. And she would be cared for and chaperoned wherever she went. Not only did Elvis swear that he loved, needed, and respected Priscilla, but he also insisted that he couldn't live without her. The Beaulieus were left with two painful alternatives: let Priscilla go and risk her being devastated if things didn't work out, or veto the proposed plan and be responsible for destroying her happiness. In the end, Elvis got his way, and Priscilla moved to Memphis.

In October 1962, while he was in Hollywood filming *Fun in Acapulco*, Elvis played host to Priscilla and her dad, and won over the senior Beaulieu with his charm and hospitality. After a few days, father and daughter flew to Memphis, where Captain Beaulieu and Vernon Presley enrolled Priscilla in the all-girl Immaculate Conception Cathedral High School and moved her into the home that Vernon shared with his second wife, Dee.

Once her father had returned to Germany, however, Priscilla seemed uncomfortable living with her future in-laws, and soon she was spending more and more time with Elvis's grandmother at Graceland. Before long, for all intents and purposes she'd basically relocated there.

Vernon chauffeured Priscilla to and from school until she got her license and he agreed to let her drive Elvis's Lincoln Mark V. He also provided her with pocket money to spend on clothes, gas, and going to the movies, bowling alley, and Leonard's Drive-In with cousin Patsy (whose mother was Gladys's sister Clettes, and father was Vernon's brother Vester). Still, despite the company of Grandma Dodger, the maids, and the secretaries, Priscilla often seemed extremely lonely waiting for Elvis to return from filming.

Priscilla was devoted to Elvis, and she followed his directives in terms of the clothes she wore, the hair that she dyed jet black to match his, and the small pearl-handled Derringer gun that she carried in her bra. She made sure that his bedroom was always set to the right temperature and his food prepared just the way he liked it. She often stayed up with him all night, watching movies or taking rides in the privately rented Memphis fairgrounds, then went to school with little or no sleep and returned home in time to bring him his mid-afternoon breakfast in bed. Dexedrine helped keep her awake. And when she

Elvis and his father celebrate Elvis's successful engagement at the International Hotel in Las Vegas in the summer of 1969. After his return to the concert stage, Elvis spent more time away from Priscilla.

needed to wind down, Elvis would give her a Placidyl.

Despite his assurances to Priscilla's parents, Elvis didn't seem all that concerned about her education. Nevertheless, he was extremely proud when she graduated from high school, and rewarded her with a red Corvair for her efforts. After graduation, Priscilla was free to spend all day, every day, with her man while he was between movie projects. Holed up in Graceland's master suite, with tin foil and blackout drapes on the windows to eliminate all sunlight, they shut themselves off from the rest of the world and spent their time talking, watching TV, having pillow fights, and making love. Still, it wasn't long before Priscilla became disturbed by the mood swings caused by the pills they were taking, so she cut down

and eventually stopped consuming them altogether. Since Elvis couldn't be persuaded to follow suit, this was the first small sign of her independence.

Depressed about the increasingly poor quality of the music and movie material with which he had to work, Elvis would often withdraw into himself, reportedly saying no one understood him, so he felt all alone. Priscilla would do her best to cheer him up, but often her efforts went unrewarded. It was a tense situation that was exacerbated by the prescription medications that Elvis was taking.

During this period of his life, Elvis sought relief for his depression through spiritual enlightenment. Accustomed to reading the ever-present Bible on his bedside table, he also began looking elsewhere

Fun at Graceland

Priscilla often endeared herself to Elvis by behaving like "one of the boys," participating in the games that he played with his entourage, although sometimes their activities were just too rough. Go-karting was high on the leisure agenda, with Elvis holding the record for the fastest time racing around Graceland's circular driveway. On one occasion, Priscilla tried to match him. Elvis clocked her on his stopwatch, smiling sweetly when she reached 15 miles per hour. She also joined in the "screaming thrill rides," when Elvis packed a bunch of people into his custom-built golf cart and raced them around the grounds at high speed. Yet, when Elvis and his friends teamed up against each other for Roman candle fights on the Fourth of July, Priscilla opted to watch all the fun from a safe distance.

for guidance, reading books such as Joseph Benner's *The Impersonal Life,* Paramahansa Yogananda's *Autobiography of a Yogi,* Kahlil Gibran's *The Prophet,* Hermann Hesse's *Siddhartha,* and Krishnamurti's *First and Last Freedom.* These books appeared to reinforce Elvis's lifelong religious beliefs and to provide him with a measure of inner peace. He often quoted from them, gave copies to friends and associates, and even held Bible readings with friends at his home in Bel Air.

In addition to expanding his horizons through literature, Elvis sought advice from Los Angeles hairdresser Larry Geller. Hired to replace Elvis's regular stylist Sal Orfice, Larry was a spiritual devotee who spent hours talking with Elvis about the commonality between all the great religions, as well as many personal issues such as why Elvis had been put on this earth; why he'd been singled out to exert such influence; why, with so many material and physical resources at his fingertips, he was so unhappy; and where he was heading. Larry introduced Elvis to the philosophical books that he devoured, as well as

Like many people who were close to the King, hairdresser Larry Geller (seen here with Elvis and Colonel Parker) later wrote about their friendship in the books If I Can Dream: Elvis' Own Story, Elvis' Search for God, *and* The Truth About Elvis.

to the Self-Realization Fellowship Center's Lake Shrine in Pacific Palisades.

Daya Mata was president of the Self-Realization Fellowship, which was founded by *Autobiography of a Yogi* author Paramahansa Yogananda. Elvis met with Mata at the organization's headquarters to learn more about using meditation to achieve a higher state of consciousness. The group's Lake Shrine inspired Elvis to create the Meditation Garden at Graceland.

As much as Elvis seemed enthused by these teachings and invigorated by his friendship with Larry Geller, others in his inner circle seemed to feel alienated or threatened. Suddenly, Elvis began to act distracted, even delusional—he would talk for hours on end with Larry Geller, and sometimes he would stare up at the stars, and claim he could perform miracles. It was said that members of the Memphis Mafia bitterly resented the hairdresser's hold over their boss, that Priscilla hated Elvis's drastically reduced interest in her,

The Wedding Dress and Suit

Elvis's wedding garb seems surprisingly subdued considering his always-ostentatious personal taste in clothing. The black brocade jacket and matching vest are made from a paisley fabric. Paisley prints, which were fashionable during the 1960s, were often loud and colorful, but the all-black fabric of Elvis's suit tempers the large pattern. Plain black trousers completed his wedding attire.

Priscilla's gown was not designed especially for her. As a matter of fact, it was purchased off the rack shortly after Elvis proposed to her. The reasons for her choice of gown had as much to do with the need for secrecy as it did with her personal tastes. If word had leaked out while wedding arrangements were being made, the press and fans might have interfered and turned a personal event into a public spectacle. Elvis and Priscilla even devised a backup plan for eloping as an additional precaution.

Priscilla did talk with a couple of seamstresses about designs, but she didn't trust them enough to tell them it was for her wedding dress. Disguised in dark glasses and a hat, Priscilla searched several exclusive shops in Memphis and Los Angeles for her dress, usually with Charlie Hodge posing as her fiancé. The story of Priscilla's wedding gown is yet another indication of the price that Elvis and his family paid for his celebrity.

and during the last year of his life he welcomed Larry Geller back to the fold.

As frustrated as she seemed by Elvis's relationship with Larry Geller, Priscilla had reason to celebrate. For the past few years, her parents had been inquiring about Elvis's intention to marry her, and more recently Colonel Parker had asked Elvis directly. One evening shortly before Christ-

Marty Lacker served as one of the best men at Elvis's wedding. His long friendship with Elvis began when the two attended L. C. Humes High School, where Lacker was on the football team.

and that Colonel Parker regarded Larry as a charlatan who was undermining his own influence over Elvis. Not too surprisingly, with so much enmity toward him, Larry's influence eventually declined, and by the spring of 1967 he was out of Elvis's life. Priscilla soon encouraged Elvis to burn many of the offending books. Although less impassioned, Elvis retained his interest in religious and spiritual philosophy,

Elvis bought Priscilla's wedding ring, a 3½-carat diamond surrounded by 20 smaller diamonds, from jeweler Harry Levitch. The jeweler and his wife flew to Las Vegas to deliver the ring and attend the wedding.

The Guest List

Aside from family members, the only people from Memphis who were invited to Elvis and Priscilla's wedding were disc jockey George Klein and jeweler Harry Levitch. They joined the small wedding party in Palm Springs, where Joe Esposito and Marty Lacker, who were already in California, were chosen to serve as Elvis's best men. Priscilla's sister Michelle was the maid of honor. The wedding party departed for Las Vegas just after midnight on May 1, flying in a couple of leased jets, and at 3:30 A.M. Elvis and Priscilla obtained a $15 marriage license. The ceremony took place at the Aladdin about six hours later. Only at the last minute did the Colonel inform most of Elvis's entourage that there was no room for them, which caused some dissent in the ranks of the Memphis Mafia, especially with bodyguard, songwriter, and longtime friend Red West, who refused to attend the subsequent reception.

mas 1966, Elvis went down on one knee in the bedroom at Graceland and proposed to Cilla. Then he slipped a ring on her finger. Purchased from jeweler Harry Levitch, the ring featured a $3^1/_2$-carat diamond encircled by a row of smaller, detachable diamonds. Just over seven years after her first meeting with Elvis, Priscilla's early fantasies became reality.

The wedding itself took place on Monday, May 1, 1967. Following his period of ranch living on the Circle G, Elvis filmed *Clambake* in Los Angeles while Colonel Parker made the wedding arrangements. The ceremony took place at the Aladdin Hotel in Las Vegas, in the small second-floor suite of the Colonel's friend, owner Milton Prell. The nuptials were presided over by Nevada Supreme Court Justice David Zenoff and took

Elvis and Priscilla are all smiles following the birth of their daughter, Lisa Marie, on February 1, 1968. The infant was given the middle name Marie to honor Colonel Tom Parker's wife, Marie.

The proud parents escort their daughter home from Baptist Memorial Hospital in Memphis.

The newlyweds spent their honeymoon in Palm Springs, and after a couple of days they returned to Memphis where, on May 29, they climbed back into their wedding attire and threw a reception at Graceland for all of their relatives, friends, and employees, as well as a few lucky fans. The only absentee was Red West, who refused to attend because he hadn't been invited to the actual wedding ceremony.

Less than two months after the wedding, Elvis began work on *Speedway*, and on July 12 he made an announcement on the set that Priscilla was pregnant. Yet, it wasn't long before rumors began to swirl that Elvis was having an affair with his costar Nancy Sinatra. Then, seven months into the pregnancy, he shocked Priscilla by suggesting that they have a trial separation. This idea was quickly dropped, but after their daughter, Lisa Marie, was born on February 1, 1968, the relationship cooled quickly. For a time, Priscilla tried to reignite the marriage, but after Elvis returned to the concert stage in the summer of 1969, his frequent lengthy absences put further strain on the already troubled relationship. In early 1972, she and Elvis separated, and their divorce was finalized on October 9, 1973. They remained friends, and even held hands during their divorce proceedings.

Though he may have been a less-than-devoted husband, there's no doubt that

less than ten minutes. In true Colonel Parker style, a press conference was held immediately afterward, followed by a breakfast reception for 100 guests, including many members of the press.

Elvis was a doting father to Lisa Marie. Until the end of his life Elvis adored Lisa Marie, spoiling her and showering her with jewels and gifts when she visited him, and rarely, if ever, disciplining her. As in many other aspects of his life, Elvis's love for his daughter ran to excess. Once, he flew her aboard his private jet so she could play in the snow. For her birthday, he rented the amusement park Libertyland for Lisa Marie and her friends. He bought her a golf cart and a pony, which he let her ride through the front door of Graceland.

In her autobiography, Priscilla asserted that she and Elvis retained their mutual affinity and relished their joint role as parents. During one of their last phone conversations, Priscilla mused over the possibility that one day it might be their time once again. "Yeah," Elvis joked, "when I'm seventy and you're sixty. We'll both be so old, we'll look really silly, racing around in golf carts."

In a 1988 interview for Life, *Lisa Marie recalled the time she spent with her father, "He was always up to something, shooting off firecrackers or guns, running around, driving golf carts or snowmobiles. . . . He called me Buttonhead or Yisa. . . . "*

Royal Duties, Regal Pleasures

Fun-loving and generous to a fault, Elvis indulged his every whim while taking care of loved ones and strangers.

Although Elvis's boredom in his later years has been well documented, there can be no doubt that he enjoyed the fruits of his success. He spent a lot of his free time in the pursuit of pleasure, and although this had its downside, it was also a very positive thing—life with Elvis often amounted to plenty of fun, even if it sometimes resembled a roller-coaster ride when he'd go to extreme lengths to fulfill his desires.

Sample the occasion in February 1976, when, sitting around at Graceland, Elvis told his friends about the incredible peanut butter and jelly sandwiches that he'd recently enjoyed at the Colorado Mine Company restaurant in Denver, when he'd visited the Mile High City to attend the funeral of a friend on the local police force. Called "Fool's Gold," these hearty snacks were trimmed with a pound of bacon and cost an astounding $49.95. As he talked about them, Elvis began working up an appetite, and soon everyone else was salivating, too. Elvis suggested a visit to the restaurant, and before his friends knew it, he had ordered up his private jet, the *Lisa Marie,* and all 19 of them were winging their way toward the Rockies.

Aboard the plane an order was placed by phone for 22 Fool's Gold sandwiches. The order was hand-delivered on the Denver Airport runway by the restaurant owner, his wife, and an employee at 1:40 A.M., and for the next couple of hours Elvis and his friends feasted on the peanut butter, jelly, and bacon sandwiches, while drinking champagne and sparkling water. Then they took to the skies once more to return to Memphis. The quickie 2,000-mile round-trip cost in excess of $16,000.

Of course, peanut butter looms large in the Presley legend courtesy of the fried peanut butter and mashed banana sandwiches that Gladys made for Elvis as a

The interior of the Lisa Marie *was extensively refurbished after Elvis purchased it in 1975. Aboard the jet, there were televisions, two couches, leather chairs, and a private bedroom with a queen-size bed.*

The Lisa Marie *required a crew of four, including captain Elwood David, copilot Ron Strauss, flight engineer Jim Manning, and flight attendant Carol Bouchere.*

It's obvious that Elvis was never into health food—he was simply interested in satisfying his desire for plenty of rich, flavorful meals, particularly Southern favorites such as meatloaf with mushroom gravy; pork chops with sweet potatoes and savory collard greens; country-fried chicken with mashed potatoes and black-eyed peas; barbecued ribs with a creamy onion casserole; rye bread sandwiches containing six slices of burnt bacon slathered with mustard; and, of course, hot dogs, hamburgers, and fries. Despite recordings such as "Song of the Shrimp" and "Do the Clam," Elvis never included fish on his menu.

Like many of Elvis's possessions, the Lisa Marie *features the TCB logo and gold lightning bolt ("Taking Care of Business in a Flash").*

child, which he continued to devour throughout his life. The peanut butter and 'nanner sandwich, as he used to call it, wasn't invented by Gladys, but it became her son's signature dish, famous for his stipulation that the toasted bread and mashed banana be embellished with a ¼-inch-thick spread of peanut butter. From an early age, Elvis had a hearty appetite—a September 1955 article in the *Country Song Roundup* quoted his then-girlfriend Dixie Locke describing how, at one sitting, she'd seen the "Hillbilly Cat" eat eight deluxe cheeseburgers and two BLT sandwiches, washed down with three chocolate milk shakes.

At Graceland, breakfast was served at all hours—sweet grits; fried cornmeal mash; corned beef, potato, and pepper hash; jelly doughnuts; eggs Benedict; blueberry corn muffins; biscuits and red-eye gravy—and so was dessert. Apple pie, cherry pie, pecan pie, blueberry pie, lemon meringue pie, sweet potato pie, banana coconut chiffon pie, and banana pudding were among Elvis's favorite treats. Elvis's passion for food, like his passion for life, was never halfhearted. When he liked something, he embraced it to his fullest capacity, whether it was a banana split or an addition to one of his many collections.

Early in his career, when he'd already taken to renting out movie theaters and theme parks late at night or in the early morning hours so that he and his friends could enjoy themselves in privacy, Elvis began indulging his taste for cars. Among the first and most famous was the eight-cylinder, four-door, custom pink 1955 Cadillac Fleetwood sedan that he reportedly gave to his mother even though she couldn't drive. A symbol of his incredible success as America's first rock 'n' roller, this was the only vehicle that Elvis kept throughout his life. Cadillacs were his favorite form of transportation, as attested to by the more than 100 such vehicles that he purchased for himself and his friends through the years, including a purple 1956 Eldorado and a 1960 Series 75 Fleetwood convertible

When Elvis wanted his new 1956 Cadillac Eldorado painted purple, he squashed a handful of grapes on the fender to indicate the exact color he wanted.

Elvis adds a little spit and polish to his 1955 Cadillac.

"King of the Kustomizers," the limo was like a mini Graceland on wheels, combining state-of-the-art gadgetry with the gaudiness and ostentation that Elvis adored. The passenger compartment and trunk were upholstered in white-pearled, leather-grained vinyl and gold crushed velvet; white sheepskin adorned the floor; and there were gold lamé curtains across the rear window and separating the front and back seats. The interior adornments and accessories were all plated in 24-carat gold, including the upholstery buttons; an engraved dashboard plaque; dual radio-telephones; a motorized shoe buffer; electric clippers; refrigerator; wet bar; and the entertainment system with its swivel-mounted color TV, RCA ten-disc auto-change record player, Kenwood AM-FM radio, Kenwood tape deck, and Kenwood multi-speaker sound system.

limousine that had to be the most outrageous of all the King's cars.

Tailored to his specifications by George Barris, Hollywood's self-proclaimed

The car's bodywork was every bit as impressive (or overbearing, depending on your point of view) as the interior. The two-tone white and gold paint comprised

40 layers of Murano pearl lacquer that featured gold swirls, diamond dust, and shimmering fish scales imported from Asia. The fenders, grille, headlight rims, wheel rims, hubcaps, and guitar-shaped it, traffic ground to a halt, and the damage caused by overzealous fans trying to touch the vehicle incurred a small fortune in repairs. Elvis was left with little choice but to lock it up inside the garage

Elvis poses with his growing collection of cars outside his Audubon Drive home.

hood ornament were all plated in 24-carat gold. The total cost to customize the limousine was around $100,000. However, the vehicle was so eye-catching that, whenever Elvis attempted to drive at his Graceland mansion to keep it in pristine condition.

The gold Cadillac was certainly unique, but there were numerous other incredible

Cadillac Fever

Just when it looked like Elvis's expensive gold Cadillac would lie forever dormant inside his garage, wily Colonel Tom Parker recouped some of the outlay and put the car to good use. In 1966, he persuaded RCA to purchase the vehicle for $24,000 and, at a time when Elvis had unofficially retired from live concerts, send it out on tour instead. So it was that the Caddy drew 40,000 fans in Houston, accepted an invitation to appear as the guest of honor at a dinner for 250 dignitaries in Atlanta, served as a parking lot attraction outside theaters screening Elvis's movies, and even toured overseas to great acclaim before being donated to Nashville's Country Music Hall of Fame.

cars among the many vehicles that Elvis bought for himself throughout his life. These included a Rolls-Royce; a three-door Messerschmidt; and a black 1973 Stutz Blackhawk III with red interior and 18-carat gold-plated trim. This was the last vehicle the King ever drove, returning to Graceland from a dentist's appointment shortly after midnight on August 16, 1977, less than 12 hours before his death.

George Barris, meanwhile, didn't only "kustomize" cars. He also turned a motor home and a tour bus into mobile palaces for the King, and worked on nine Triumph 650 motorcycles in early 1965 when Elvis, a confirmed Harley-Davidson fan, was impressed by Jerry Schilling's 650 and wanted one for himself and several of his friends. During the same period, Elvis also bought cars for his entire entourage, and this became a lifelong trend, not only in terms of the gifts that he gave to family and friends, but also those that he handed over to complete strangers. On one occasion, while buying Eldorados for two members of the Memphis Mafia, his heart went out to a young couple who were walking around the dealership, looking for a car they could afford. After telling them to pick any vehicle they wanted, he wrote out a check and asked the salesperson to take care of the paperwork. Still, this was small potatoes when compared to his later generosity.

On July 27, 1975, Elvis bought and gave away no fewer than 13 Cadillacs. And

On July 27, 1975, during a buying spree at a Memphis Cadillac dealership, Elvis spotted bank teller Mennie Person admiring his vehicle and impulsively purchased a Cadillac for her.

An Unusual "Collection"

In 1956 or early 1957, a rumor ran rampant that insisted Elvis collected teddy bears. Fanzines were thrilled at the contradiction that this bit of news seemed to indicate. What would a notorious, swivel-hipped rock 'n' roller be doing with a collection of teddy bears? It was fodder for fanzines and reporters for months. Fans sent Elvis teddy bears by the hundreds, which he in turn donated to children's hospitals or organizations such as the National Foundation for Infantile Paralysis. Publicity was generated about his generosity, which prompted more teddy bears from his fans. A more perfect publicity gimmick could not have been invented.

Conveniently, the Colonel mentioned Elvis's alleged hobby in an interview on January 24, 1957—the very day that Elvis recorded the song "Teddy Bear" for the soundtrack of *Loving You.* The publicity about Elvis's extensive teddy bear collection didn't hurt the song's chances of hitting the top of the charts, which it did in July 1957.

when he saw his own limousine being admired in front of the Memphis dealership by a bank teller named Mennie Person, he bought her a Cadillac *and* threw in a check for new clothes to go with her acquisition. That little splurge cost more than $140,000. But then, 1975 was a big year for Elvis's spending sprees. That December, during a trip to Colorado, he spent around $70,000 on Cadillacs and Lincolns for his police buddies and their wives. When Don Kinney, the host of KOA-TV's *Denver Today,* heard about this, he joked on-air that he didn't want a big Cadillac, just "one of those little sporty ones." Minutes later he received a call from Elvis: A brand-new Seville was waiting for him at the dealership. Such acts of generosity were not only hard to

explain, but they would also become the stuff of legend.

Cars weren't Elvis's only source of pleasure during that spend, spend, spend period. In April 1975, he purchased a 1958 Convair 880 aircraft for $250,000, spent more than $800,000 to refurbish it, and renamed it the *Lisa Marie* in honor of his daughter. Capable of seating 28 passengers, the jet afforded him a bedroom with queen-size bed and closed-circuit TV; a conference room with a quadraphonic eight-track system and international sky phone; a lounge with oversized sofas and chairs, and gold-plated seat belt buckles; and two half-baths where the sinks were made with flecks of 24-carat gold.

Elvis (top row, 2nd from left) loved football, and during the early 1960s he formed his own Elvis Presley Enterprises football team to play private matches in Memphis and Los Angeles.

In July, Elvis purchased a Grumman Gulfstream G–1 airplane for Colonel Parker, and then a couple of months later he spent just under $900,000 on a ten-passenger Lockheed JetStar. Though smaller than the *Lisa Marie*, this plane housed an oven, bar, bathroom, three tables, and a Sony stereo system, as well as a pilot named Milo High. (Even Elvis's corniest movie characters would have been hard-pressed to outdo that moniker.)

Back on terra firma, personal physician George Nichopolous introduced Elvis to the wonders of racquetball in the hope that his increasingly out-of-shape patient might be inspired to get fit. Elvis took an instant liking to the sport and—urged on by Dr. Nick—he built a two-story, 2,240-square-foot racquetball building behind the main house at Graceland. The court was augmented by a fully furnished first-floor lounge with a piano, stereo system, half-bath, and glass viewing wall behind

In earlier, healthier times, Elvis loved the rough and tumble of football. Initially, the Cleveland Browns were his favorite football team, and he later followed the Pittsburgh Steelers. He'd watch three games at once on the trio of sets in the TV room at Graceland, and during the early 1960s he even formed his own Elvis Presley Enterprises football team, which sometimes played private matches in stadiums that he rented in Memphis and Los Angeles. Nevertheless, the great

Elvis initially studied karate in the Army, but it wasn't until the late 1960s that he took formal training.

Elvis loved the spiritual aspects of studying karate, and also incorporated many moves into his live stage act.

the court. Upstairs, another lounge offered a weight equipment workout area, bar, refrigerator, pinball machine, guest showers, and a private suite for Elvis that contained a lounge area with a massage table, and a bathroom with a Jacuzzi whirlpool tub and five-head shower/ steam bath.

sporting love of his life was karate, which he began studying while in the Army. Following his discharge, Elvis decided to take it more seriously, immersing himself in its spiritual as well as physical aspects, and to that end he began discussing technique with Hawaiian kenpo karate master Ed Parker. Still, it wasn't until the end of the 1960s that Elvis turned to him for formal training, and then it was to develop skills that he could use to defend himself should he ever be threatened by a member of the public, and also to provide him with moves that could be incorporated into his stage act.

Eventually, Priscilla also studied with Ed Parker at his Los Angeles studio. Parker in turn recommended that, when they were in Memphis, the Presleys should take instruction from Korean-born Kang Rhee, a specialist in the tae kwon do form of karate that focused on hand and leg speed. No sooner had Elvis signed on with Master Rhee, than several of his sidekicks signed on, too, including Red and Sonny West, Jerry Schilling, George Klein, and Charlie Hodge. Elvis reportedly became obsessed with demonstrating his prowess on the mat, even if it meant using a little persuasion to ensure that Ed Parker awarded him a sixth-degree black belt in kenpo karate. Kang Rhee subsequently awarded Elvis a seventh-degree black belt in the Pasaryu system, and soon the avid student was working with both masters to get to the next level.

Elvis's heightened passion for the sport coincided with the worldwide kung fu craze of the early 1970s, and he watched techniques employed on-screen by the likes of Bruce Lee and David Chow while planning to star in his own action movie. Although this dream never materialized, his interest in karate continued. Martial arts helped project the machismo that

Quite a Show

Elvis's karate skills came in handy during a midnight concert in Las Vegas on February 20, 1973. Four drunken fans rushed the stage, and after bodyguard Red West intercepted one of the men, Elvis assumed a karate stance and knocked a second fan off the stage and into the audience. Highly agitated, he was ready to take on all four men. However, Vernon Presley and the Colonel's assistant, Tom Diskin, calmed Elvis down, and once the show resumed he issued an apology...of sorts. "I'm sorry, ladies and gentlemen," he remarked. "I'm sorry I didn't break his goddamn neck is what I'm sorry about." Roaring its appreciation, the crowd gave Elvis a standing ovation.

Elvis had a lifelong respect and fascination for law enforcement officials. Here, he poses with actor Nick Adams (left) and Memphis police Captain Fred Woodward.

their meeting, Elvis sent President Nixon a handwritten letter in which he condemned subversives and the hippie-related drug culture, and offered to use his considerable influence to combat drug abuse and communist brainwashing techniques should he be made an honorary federal agent. Before receiving his

had always been a strong part of Elvis's persona, and which was also reflected in another of his pastimes: collecting guns and police paraphernalia.

Surrounded by police and security officials since the earliest days of fan hysteria, Elvis was often presented with complimentary badges and was inducted into several law enforcement organizations. When Elvis asked Roy Nixon, the sheriff of Shelby County, Tennessee (where Graceland was located), to furnish Elvis, Vernon, and numerous members of the Memphis Mafia with official deputy sheriff's badges, Sheriff Nixon duly obliged. On December 21, 1970, Elvis hastily requested—and was granted—a meeting with President Richard Nixon in the White House Oval Office, which resulted in Nixon presenting him with a federal narcotics officer's badge. Prior to

Elvis received an honorary deputy sheriff's badge in Lee County, Mississippi.

badge, Elvis gave the Secret Service a gift for the President: a commemorative World War II Colt .45 pistol encased in a wooden box, similar to the turquoise-handled Colt .45 that was a favorite in the King's own collection.

Other guns in Elvis's collection included a huge .44 magnum; a Python .357 pistol with the TCB/lightning logo ("Taking Care of Business in a Flash") engraved just above the handle; a Colt .45 automatic that Elvis would sometimes stick in his belt; and a small pearl-handled Derringer that he'd pack in his boot or strap to his leg, arming himself against the death and kidnapping threats that he received on a regular basis after returning to the concert stage in 1969. As it happens, the Derringer was reportedly only put to really effective use when Elvis became agitated by what, or whom, he saw on television. In one infamous incident, the

At a visit with President Nixon in the Oval Office, Elvis was presented with a badge from the U.S. Bureau of Narcotics.

An Impromptu Performance

Just after 4:00 in the morning on August 16, 1977, Elvis picked up the phone in the master suite at Graceland and called his cousin Billy Smith to ask if he and his wife, Jo, wanted to play racquetball. The Smiths had been sleeping, but they agreed to join Elvis and his girlfriend, Ginger Alden, for a workout in the racquetball building. Once there, Jo and Ginger played for a while, followed by Billy and Elvis, and when Elvis quickly ran out of steam all four of them retired to the lower lounge. Sitting at the piano, Elvis played and sang several numbers, including "Unchained Melody" and "Blue Eyes Crying in the Rain." As the other three sat and relaxed, none of them realized they had just witnessed Elvis Presley's final musical performance.

appearance of singer Robert Goulet on Elvis's television was enough for him to blow the screen to smithereens.

There was rarely a dull moment at the court of the King.

Firearms Collection

Elvis's interest in guns remains a controversial aspect of his persona. Detractors like to recount the stories of his irresponsibility with guns, most of which have been exaggerated through retelling in countless books. Many of these stories originated in biographies by former employees and associates who had an ax to grind, so some of their "memories of Elvis" are dubious at best. The incident where Elvis shot out his television screen because Robert Goulet was singing, for instance, has been exaggerated over time into a version in which Elvis shot out the screen every time he saw Robert Goulet, or any singer he didn't like, on TV.

Elvis's interest in firearms dates back to his youth, though it is often wrongly attributed to his depressed, drug-induced state from the 1970s.

Despite the hyperbole, Elvis was not a mere fan of firearms; he was a fanatic. Occasionally plagued by death threats during the 1970s, he took to wearing a derringer strapped to his leg while he was performing. When he attended private showings of James Bond movies, he liked to carry his Walther PPK because that was the weapon issued to 007. As he grew more despondent in the last few years of his life, his misadventures with guns increased, casting a dark shadow over a troubled man.